DEATH BY
CHILLI SAUCE

First published in 2012 by Old Street Publishing Ltd`
Trebinshun House, Brecon LD3 7PX

www.oldstreetpublishing.co.uk

ISBN 978-1-906964-95-5

10 9 8 7 6 5 4 3 2 1

A CIP catalogue record for this title is available from the British Library.

DEATH BY
CHILLI SAUCE

*The Remarkable Truth
and Surprising Science behind
101 Memorable Movie Moments*

RICHARD GERMAIN

CONTENTS

OBJECTS

NATURE

TRANSPORT

WEAPONRY

FOOD AND DRINK

BEASTS

CRIME

FOREWORD

"Strange things happen all the time."
Blue Velvet

There are those who'll tell you that Hollywood is a ridiculous, away-with-the-fairies place where people can jump from improbable heights, where guns never run out of bullets, where there's always a parking space when you need one (and you never have to lock your car), and where one in every set of identical twins is born pure evil.

They'll also delight in informing you that movie directors are no better than charlatans, ignoring as they do the laws of physics, commonsense and just about everything else, and assuming that we – the cinema-going shmucks – will believe whatever they show us.

In short, these people will tell you that Hollywood is hokum.

But I don't believe that moviemakers are as stupid as they look – although baseball caps really shouldn't be worn by anyone over the age of 18. So I've taken 101 memorable movie moments – from the sublime to the ridiculous, from John Huston to John Hughes – to see whether directors are guilty of hijacking reality. Or whether what we see on the screen can actually happen in real life.

It's been a voyage of strange discoveries, from finding out whether tumbleweed actually exists outside westerns to learning whether maggots really do help to heal a wound (not to mention whether chilli sauce can kill you). I want to know, 'Could that happen in real life?', 'What the hell is that all about?' and 'I bet Chaplin couldn't really light a match on the seat of his pants.'

A word of warning: **these pages may contain plot spoilers.** If you don't want to know what happens in a film, it may be a good idea to skip forward to the next entry.

EASY TO SWALLOW))))) **IMPOSSIBLE TO SWALLOW**

HUMANKIND

"That day for no particular
reason, I decided to go for a
little run."

Forrest Gump

FORREST GUMP

(1994, Dir. Robert Zemeckis)

The bit where Forrest jogs non-stop for three years, two months

Run Forrest run! And indeed he did. For over three years, everyone's favourite half-wit pounded the tarmac from sea to shining sea, whilst at the same time growing a beard, creating globally-adopted slogans and inventing jogging. We presume he stopped to sleep and we hope he stopped when nature called. But with the film showing at least four crossings of the States (around 18,000 km in total, depending on where you cross), it's still a long, long way.

And it's possible. Real-life Forrest Gumps are out there. They're called ultra-distance runners, and some seem to be even more foolish than their fictional counterpart. Take the annual Self-Transcendence 3,100 Mile Race in New York. Its organisers describe it as the world's longest footrace. And with a course of 3,100 miles (4,989 km) few would argue.

So how do they squeeze nearly 5,000 km out of New York? By having competitors run 5,649 laps of one city block in Queens. And to make things even less fun, the race takes part between June and August, when New York is at its hottest. The 2011 race was won by a Ukranian, Sarvagata Ukrainskyi, who completed the course in 44 days (that's 70 miles a day).

Seriously impressive. But 44 days is not three years. For that kind of time on the hoof we need to turn to a Dane called Jesper Olsen, the first person to run around the world. He completed the 26,000 km (16,155 miles) between 1 January 2004 and 23 October 2005 at an average of 28 miles a day (a marathon is 26 miles). But that wasn't enough. Jesper is currently engaged on World Run II, a little jaunt across four continents starting at Europe's most northern point, Nordkapp in Norway; then down

to the southernmost tip of South Africa, Cape Agulhas; across to Punta Arenas, the southern tip of Argentina; and finally up to the northwestern tip of Newfoundland in Canada. With a distance of 40,000 km (24,854 miles) in 800 days, World Run II is the longest, 'non-stop' GPS-documented run… by a very long way.

At the time of writing, Jesper has run nearly 35,000 km and is somewhere in the USA. So, come on Jesp – get a shuffle on! To quote the great man himself (Jesper not Forrest): "I think that the ability to run incomprehensible distances is a thing we all share as humans. It's not the talent of a few extreme individuals. We have had thousands of years of evolution where it was normal to be in motion all the day long. Only within the last few centuries has it become normal to sit down most of the day." So off your backside and into your tracksuit. Who's for a little race?

Chilli Sauce Score: ♪

BE KIND REWIND

(2008, Dir. Michel Gondry)

The bit where Jack Black becomes magnetized

It's a film about making films. When Jerry (Jack Black) breaks into an electrical substation (never a good idea) and becomes magnetized (told you), his mere presence in his friend's video rental store causes every VHS tape to erase itself. No more *Ghostbusters*, *Rush Hour 2* or *Driving Miss Daisy*. So Jerry is forced to re-shoot the films on a shoe-string budget and with the lowest of lo-fi effects. There's no technological jiggery-pokery in Jerry's oeuvre – but what about the magnetic field flowing from his fleshy form?

First, only a few substances, such as iron, become magnetized themselves after being subjected to a magnetic field. And the quantity of these 'ferromagnets' in the human body is far too small to have the nearest drawer of cutlery attaching itself to one's forehead. Yet that doesn't stop many people from *claiming* to be magnetized, nor from "experts" backing them up. Take Leonid Tenkaev, a Russian factory worker, his wife Galina, their daughter Tanya and grandson Kolya. In 1987, one year after the Chernobyl disaster, the Tenkaev family found that metal objects would stick to their bodies. And they got a doctor to prove it: "There is absolutely no doubt that the objects stick as if their bodies were magnetic," said Dr Atusi Kono in 1991.

Other human magnets – and there are many: 300 of them once attended a "Superfields" conference in Bulgaria – say they can attract different materials such as glass, wood and plastic. And this hints at the probable truth of the matter: people can't be magnetic, but they can be sticky.

Romanian Aurel Raileanu once contacted *The Sun* newspaper about his magnetic abilities (obviously looking to attract

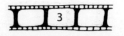

3

something a bit more remunerative than glass and wood). They took him to a magnetism expert, who used a Gauss meter to measure the magnetic field around Aurel's body. There was none. Then they visited a prominent paranormal sceptic, Christopher French of the University of London, to see if he could supply the answer. He could: sebum. When Prof. French put talcum powder on Aurel's skin, the Romanian's mysterious power of attraction immediately vanished. "When I dusted it on Aurel's chest," said Prof. French, "I found afterwards that objects slipped off. It seems to me that Aurel's ability to hold things on his chest and face is down to the stickiness of his skin, caused by the amount of a thing called sebum produced in glands."

So it looks like humans can't be magnetized. But they can be in need of a good bath.

Chilli Sauce Score: 〕〕〕〕

TARZAN THE APE MAN

(1932, Dir. W. S. Van Dyke)

The bit where Tarzan yells

Johnny Weissmuller won five Olympic gold medals and set sixty-seven swimming world records. As Tarzan, a role he played in twelve films, he swung through the trees with the greatest of ease, wrestled pretty much everything in the animal kingdom, and managed to woo the delightful Maureen O'Sullivan despite having no knowledge of the English language and certainly no idea about dressing to impress. Oh, and Johnny found time to wade his way through five marriages in real life too. But perhaps his most extraordinary legacy is that yell: part yodel, part ululation, it was enough to bring a herd of elephants to his side or to scatter his enemies to the hills.

And no one is quite sure how it was done, or indeed who did it. You'd think it would be a simple case of asking Weissmuller. But the great man seemed to change his story as often as he changed his wife. For years he claimed that the yell was his own voice and that he had developed it out of the yodeling he had done as a child; after all, he was born in what was Austria-Hungary.

However, on an American daytime talk show in the 1970s (how the mighty fall), Weissmuller said that the yell was created by mixing the recordings of a soprano, an alto... and a hog caller. And he was also known to tell a story of being in Cuba in 1959 when the revolution was in full swing. Castro's men ambushed Weissmuller's car when he was on the way to a celebrity golf tournament (I'm not making this up). Our Johnny convinced the gun-toting soldiers that he wasn't fighting for the other side (or indeed for anyone) by giving the famous yell. The soldiers

immediately recognised the star and allowed him to continue – though what he carded on the golf course later that day is unfortunately not known.

So, he yelled the yell. Then he didn't. And then he sort of did again. Others have their own stories. Johnny Sheffield, who played Boy in the Tarzan films and had his own yell, remembered giving a voice sampling which was enhanced to produce his cry. But he was unsure whether the same was done for Weissmuller. One film editor claimed that the yell was a layered mix created from Weissmuller's voice, the sound of a violin's G-string, the bleat of a camel, the growl of a dog and the howl of a hyena. Samuel Marx, in his book on Hollywood *Mayer and Thalberg: The Make-Believe Saints* (Random House, 1975), ventured that the cry was electronically enhanced and then run backwards. Indeed, the sound can be shown to be palindromic – that is, the same forwards and backwards.

But just as it seems we're getting close to the truth, up pops Johnny Sheffield again to say that when Weissmuller moved studios to RKO he recorded a new yell which Sheffield was sure was Johnny's own. And maybe this was the yell that has been trademarked by Edgar Rice Burroughs, Inc. Sound trademark serial no. 75326989 is described as 'consisting of a series of approximately ten sounds, alternating between the chest and falsetto registers of the voice.'

Did Weissmuller actually produce the famous noise for real in his films? Well, maybe. At any rate, trying to uncover the truth was enough to make me, well, yell.

Chilli Sauce Score:)))

SHUTTER ISLAND

(2010, Dir. Martin Scorcese)

The bit where mentally-ill patients undergo lobotomies

 Shutter Island is an anagram of both 'Truths and Lies' and 'Truths/Denials'. And that tells you a lot about this gothic thriller starring Scorcese favourite Leonardo DiCaprio as Teddy Daniels, a US Marshal investigating the disappearance of a patient at Ashecliffe Hospital for the criminally insane on the storm-lashed Shutter Island. It's an atmospheric, twisting and unsettling film that shows Scorcese's masterly control of every aspect of film-making. Nothing can be taken for granted in or on Shutter Island – especially with Sir Ben Kingsley as the hospital's head of psychiatry, Max von Sydow as a mysterious German doctor and a rumour of lobotomies being performed in a lighthouse.

But was the removal of part of a patient's brain really seen as a sensible way of curing them?

You'd have thought that if you were suffering from chronic headaches or mental illness, the last thing you'd want is someone drilling a hole in your head. Yet a technique known as trepanning is one of the earliest surgical procedures known to man. Although it doesn't generally involve the removal of brain matter, trepanning has been used for thousands of years to cure pain and epilepsy. The theory was that boring a hole in the skull enabled evil spirits to escape. Numerous trepanned skulls have been found, including a male skull from around 5100 B.C. which shows two partially-healed holes, indicating that the man lived for several years afterwards – and without anaesthetics or antiseptics. Ouch.

Incidentally, the practice still goes on, although nowadays it tends, even more gruesomely, to be self-trepanning. There are those out there – visit the International Trepanation Advocacy Group's website if you don't believe me – who think that giving your head a sunroof increases blood flow and therefore vitality and creativity. Just ask group-founder Peter Halvorson, who opened up a blowhole in the front of his skull with a drill.)

In the 19th century, the first serious attempt at what is termed psychosurgery was undertaken by Swiss psychiatrist Gottlieb Burckhardt, who operated on six mentally-ill patients in 1888. Even the most generous of observers would say that the results were mediocre: one patient died after five days, one committed suicide, two showed no improvement and the last two became 'quieter'.

It wasn't until the 1930s that psychosurgery was transformed from creepy experiment to legitimate treatment. But it remained pretty gruesome. In 1935, Portuguese António Egas Moniz performed what he called a 'leucotomy' on a mentally-ill patient by drilling holes in the skull and injecting alcohol to destroy brain tissue. A year later, American Walter Freeman took up the drill and renamed the procedure 'lobotomy'. If anyone could be called Mr Lobotomy, Freeman was he. It was Freeman who invented the transorbital lobotomy in 1946. Those of a squeamish disposition might want to look away now because this involved, first, electric-shocking the patient into unconsciousness, then taking a miniature ice pick and inserting it above the eyeball, through the eye socket and into the frontal lobes of the brain. The ice pick was then manoeuvred around to scramble the neural connections.

Freeman would perform 2,500 lobotomies during his career, out of a total of 100,000 performed worldwide from the 1930s to the 1970s, when more effective treatments made the procedure obsolete. One of the more famous recipients of a lobotomy was Rosemary Kennedy, the sister of the president. She was believed to be mentally retarded by her father Joseph but this analysis has since been disputed. Indeed Rosemary seems to have been a fully-functioning person with an active social life. She did, however, suffer vicious mood swings, and it was this that led to her undergoing a Walter Freeman lobotomy in 1941. The mood swings disappeared but so did much of Rosemary's personality.

She became infantile, incontinent and unintelligible, and would stare blankly at walls for hours. She lived another sixty-four years, dying in 2005 at the age of 86.

Although lobotomies have had the chop, an operation called a hemispherectomy is sometimes performed on patients who suffer severe seizures as a result of infection, trauma or tumours. And as the name suggests, a hemispherectomy involves the removal of half the brain. The procedure, which takes up to twelve hours, is most effective when performed on younger patients, as children's brains are better able to adapt, with the remaining half of the brain taking over some of the lost side's functions. Some paralysis to the side of the body opposite to the removed hemisphere always occurs. But the patient's intellect is rarely affected and indeed is is often enhanced as the patient no longer suffers seizures.

When it comes to psychosurgery, nothing can top Mike the Chicken. On 10 September 1945, Mike's owner Lloyd Olsen took an axe to the chicken's head in the expectation of a tasty dinner. Mike's head was severed but, crucially, the blade missed Mike's jugular as well as much of his brain stem. And so Mike the "Headless Wonder Chicken" picked himself up, dusted himself down and lived for another eighteen months (Mr Olsen clearly having lost his appetite). Fed by means of an eyedropper down his neck, Mike grew from two pounds in weight to nearly eight pounds, and even found time to go on a national tour with his owner-turned-manager.

In true celebrity fashion, Mike's demise occurred in the middle of the night, from choking on a piece of corn that had become lodged in his oesophagus. But at least fame didn't go to his head.

Chilli Sauce Score: *)*

ESCAPE TO ATHENA

(1979, Dir. George P. Cosmatos)

The bit where Stefanie Powers swims underwater for a very long time

 It was improbable enough to have Sonny Bono, William Holden, Elliot Gould and David Niven imprisoned together in a World War II German P.O.W. camp on a Greek island. And Roger Moore strained credulity a good deal further in his role as Austrian camp commandant and antiquarian, Major Otto Hecht. But what about Stefanie Powers' ability to swim underwater, equipped with neither air tank nor snorkel, for what, frankly, feels like ages?

Playing stripper Dottie del Mar, Ms. Powers (or Stefania Zofia Federkiewicz to give her her birth name) exhibits a fine pair of lungs. And when she dives, she also gives a good demonstration of the mammalian diving reflex, which allows some animals to dive to lung-crushing depths for prolonged periods of time. One aspect of this reflex is bradycardia. Bradycardia doesn't mean getting chest pains whenever *The Brady Bunch* comes on TV. Rather, it's the ability of the brain to slow the heart rate when it detects that the body has been immersed in water. And a lower heart rate means less oxygen is required.

Freedivers – who dive underwater while holding their breath – use this principle, which allows them to spend surprising lengths of time *sub aqua*. They have their own worldwide federation, AIDA, which oversees record attempts in the sport. The particular record we're interested in here is static apnea, in which the freediver holds their breath for as long as possible. So can anyone match Stefanie's powers? Well nearly, it seems: in 2009 one Stéphane Mifsud from France held his breath for a record-breaking, heart-stopping 11 min. 35 sec.

Yet Stéphane must have let out a (very long) sigh when he heard about Hungarian David Merlini, who was lowered into a water tank on the start line of the 2009 Bahrain Grand Prix and stayed there for 21 min. 29 sec. Merlini undoubtedly breathed quite a few lungfuls of pure oxygen before being dunked in the water – as you might have guessed from his name, he's a professional escape artist, which is why he's not recognised as the record holder.

All the same, it's enough to make you gasp.

Chilli Sauce Score: ♪♪

THE SOCIAL NETWORK

(2010, Dir. David Fincher)

The bit where Zuckerberg says there are more geniuses in China than people in the US

The Social Network is clever, fast-talking and energetic, but with about the same emotional depth as a puddle. Very similar, in fact, to Facebook founder Mark Zuckerberg as portrayed by Jesse Eisenberg. The film chronicles the birth of the online leviathan, which began life as a social networking website for Harvard College students. Zuckerberg himself has stated that much of the film is only loosely based on the facts, although they did manage to get his clothing right. So how true is it to say, as Eisenberg does in the opening scene, that there "are more people with genius IQs living in China than there are people of any kind living in the United States"?

How do you define genius? You could say that a person who is very, very intelligent is a genius, in which case the definition of genius can be linked in a straightforward way to a person's Intelligence Quotient (IQ). Yet many people believe that intelligence and genius, though related, are not the same thing. Genius seems to encompass something greater than "mere" intelligence, including elements of creativity, ingenuity and productivity. In other words, no one can be called a genius who hasn't achieved something very impressive indeed. Think Leonardo da Vinci.

But for all its limitations, the IQ test does at least give us something reasonably quantifiable to work with (indeed, some schools use the test to identify gifted children who might require special education). There is more than one recognised IQ test, but they all tend to measure a person's memory and language, and their spatial and mathematical abilities. They're also designed so that the majority of people score between 90 and 110. But what about geniuses?

Mensa, the high-IQ society, doesn't actually give an IQ score above which you're eligible to join. Instead, it accepts those who achieve a score that is on or above the 98th percentile (i.e. a score that is better than those of at least 98% of the general population). This works out as an IQ of roughly 148. And among the wise guys and gals who are believed to be Mensa members (the organisation doesn't publish a membership list) there have been a few surprises, including Sir Jimmy Saville (showing that brain power doesn't extend to fashion sense), former Leyton Orient footballer Andy Harris (showing that you can be a genius on or off the pitch – though perhaps not both), and former Playboy Playmate Dr. Julie Peterson (showing that you can't judge a book by its rather scantily-clad cover).

So, to the Chinese. Well, there are around 1,356,000,000 people in China (give or take a few hundred thousand). And there are 313,500,000 Americans. It doesn't take a genius to work out that it's extremely unlikely that there are 313 million geniuses in a Chinese population of 1.3 billion because that would be (roughly) one in every four people.

But don't be disappointed. There are many other statistics about China that are as real as they are astonishing. Here are just three:

China makes 80% of the world's toys.

The Chinese smoke 50,000 cigarettes every second.

China has 64 million vacant homes, including whole cities.

But it's just not true that a quarter of Chinese people are geniuses.

Chilli Sauce Score:)))))

KENNY

(2006, Dir. Clayton Jacobson)

The bit where Kenny becomes desensitized to a smell after seven seconds

No wonder Melbourne portaloo supremo Kenny Smyth does a roaring trade. From "There's a smell in here that will outlast religion" to "It's as silly as a bum full of smarties," he's a rich source of hilarious one-liners. But Kenny also knows everything there is to know about "waste management", including the supposed fact that when you're exposed to an odour you can smell it for seven seconds before you become desensitized.

This is called sensory adaptation. The olfactory system does indeed become unable to distinguish a particular smell as the receptors in the upper region of the nose are fatigued by the odour through repeated or prolonged exposure. In fact, an odour's intensity becomes weakened after only a few breaths.

Although this is no doubt of great benefit to anyone employed in the fecal industry, it's the opposite for some other professions. The Sense of Smell Institute in New York, which describes itself as "a leading global resource relating to the sense of smell and its importance to human psychology, behavior and quality of life", advises perfumers that no more than three fragrances should be tested at one time to avoid fatigue. Similarly, wine tasters usually only take short sniffs, with regular breaks, because sensory adaptation means that a wine's perceived scent can change rapidly.

So whether sensory adaptation is a good thing or not depends what type of smelly stuff you're dealing with. But if you work in a similar profession to Kenny, it's certainly not to be sniffed at.

Chilli Sauce Score: 🌶

DIAMONDS ARE FOREVER

(1971, Dir. Guy Hamilton)

The bit where Bond says redheads have terrible tempers

 Connery is back (apparently George Lazenby's agent told him: "Don't sign a seven-movie deal; Bond is on his way out.") Much like Las Vegas, where much of it is set, *Diamonds are Forever* is silly and camp in places, but still manages to entertain. Bond is on the tail of his old nemesis Blofeld and a ring of diamond smugglers, including the delightful, redheaded Tiffany Case. According to 007, Tiffany's colouring is a sign of a hot temper. But was he being fair?

Well, given that Connery wore a toupee in all of his outings as Bond, he's hardly one to talk. But he's not the only one to generalize about those whose heads are red. Mark Twain sugested that "While the rest of the species is descended from apes, redheads are descended from cats", and a Russian proverb warns that "There was never a saint with red hair." But can these generalizations really apply to people as different as Winston Churchill, Ronald McDonald, Vincent Van Gogh, Orphan Annie and Henry VIII?

Why is red hair red? Hair colour is caused by two types of pigment called eumelanin (dark pigment) and phaeomelanin (light and reddish pigment). A single gene, MC1R, has been identified as being responsible for the mix of pigments that results in red hair. For a person to be born with red hair, they need both their parents to carry the gene, something the parents can do without being redheaded themselves. Around 4% of the world's population has red hair, which doesn't sound like much until you consider that it works out at over 280 million people. And at 13%, Scotland has the highest proportion of redheads of any country.

Other than from being thought to be hot-headed, descended

from cats and unsaintly, people with red hair are subject to some pretty strange rumours and prejudices. For instance, you should let neither eye nor shadow of a redheaded woman fall on you unless you want a big heap of bad luck. Yet if you walk between two redheaded girls, you'll end up with a bundle of cash. Some say that redheaded people make bad-tasting butter, whilst others in the 16th century believed that the fat of a redheaded man was an essential ingredient of effective poison.

In Donegal in Ireland, if a girl has red hair it means there was a pig under the bed when she was born – a common occurrence, evidently. Considerably worse, in Ancient Egypt redheaded women were sacrificed in order to rid the land of the unlucky colour. Cain was believed to have had red hair, as was Judas Iscariot – and, in the Sistine Chapel, Michelangelo depicted Eve being handed an apple by a redheaded serpent woman.

So are there any facts buried within the flummery? Not really. Some scientific studies seem to suggest that, owing to the MC1R gene, redheads are more sensitive to pain and are resistant to some anaesthetics. And that's about it. So, although a redhead might be marginally more likely to wake up furious in the middle of an operation, there's absolutely no evidence to suggest that their tempers are any more terrible (or that their characters any better or worse) than anyone else's.

And there I shall rest my (Tiffany) Case.

Chilli Sauce Score: $)))))$

SAW III

(2006, Dir. Darren Lynn Bousman)

The bit where a man tears his skin off when it freezes to a metal pipe

At the time of writing there are seven films in the *Saw* franchise. If you haven't seen any of them, here's all you need to know: a dying man called the Jigsaw Killer forces victims to play "games" which test their will to live whilst they are psychologically and physically tortured. (Nice.) Even after Jigsaw is killed in *Saw III*, the games – and the films – continue. The seventh film is in 3D… which says a lot about the direction the series is going.

In *Saw III* one unfortunate fellow gets his face frozen to a pipe. Now, technically it isn't his skin that has stuck but moisture on his cheek that has frozen and bound his face to the pipe. Thermal conductivity is the principle involved. Metal has a high thermal conductivity, meaning that, when cold, metal will remove heat from warmer materials. For moisture on the skin to freeze, the metal must be below 0°C. It can then extract heat from the moisture and lower the moisture's temperature to freezing point.

However, skin is continuously supplied with heat by circulating blood. So the metal needs to have a high enough thermal conductivity to remove heat from the moisture (thereby keeping the moisture frozen) faster than it can be supplied by the skin and blood. Unfortunately for characters trapped in a horror "threequel", the thermal conductivity of metal is first-class.

That's not the case for all materials. Plastic, paper, wood… these can all be chilled down to the minus hundreds and you won't stick to them because they can't extract heat fast enough. So if you're going to be caught up in a sadistic killer's twisted games,

make sure it takes place in a tree house.

If you do find yourself frozen to metal, some warm water will release you. How you get some is another matter entirely.

Chilli Sauce Score:)

MONTY PYTHON'S
THE MEANING OF LIFE

(1983, Dir. Terry Jones)

The bit where Mr Creosote eats so much that he bursts

Surely never in the history of pretty much anything can eating a wafer-thin mint have had such an explosively repulsive effect. Okay, it wasn't just the mint: Terry Jones' fat diner has already polished off moules marinières, pâté de foie gras, beluga caviar, eggs benedict, a leek tart and frogs' legs amandine, all mixed together in a bucket with the quails' eggs on top and a double helping of pâté.

So, can you eat so much that you explode? Studies have been undertaken to see how much the stomach can hold. These include one by a Frenchman called E. Revilloid in 1885. Revilloid filled up a stomach that had been removed from a deceased person until it ruptured. It took 4,000cc of liquid to do so. In 1891, a Swedish physician called Key-Åberg repeated the experiment but left the stomach inside its dead owner. It took the same 4,000 cc to rupture the stomach. As far as we know, the stiff remained ... well, stiff, and did not itself explode.

Some stomachs seem to be able to find room for much more, including that of a 23-year-old Londoner – not a food critic, a trucker or professional darts player, but a fashion model. According to the April 1985 issue of medical journal *The Lancet*, the young woman sat down and worked her way through 19 pounds of food, including one pound of liver, two pounds of kidney, a half pound steak, one pound of cheese, two eggs, two thick slices of bread, one cauliflower, ten peaches, four pears, two apples, four bananas, two pounds each of plums, carrots and grapes, and two glasses of milk. Her stomach couldn't find

room for it all and ruptured, releasing trillions of bacteria which poisoned and killed her.

The unfortunate truth was that the woman was bulimic and her stomach had been weakened by periods of starvation. Similarly, in a 1947 issue of the *British Medical Journal*, the surgeon commander of the Polish Navy described the cases of four prisoners-of-war who had been starved, but on release had eaten until their stomachs burst, with one man consuming a relatively modest two quarts of soup, one quart of coffee, half a pound of bread and some potatoes over the course of a day.

However, the only recorded case of someone exploding through over-eating is actually the case of a something – a 13-foot Burmese python which attempted to swallow a 6-foot alligator whole. The remains of the two beasts were found by rangers in the Everglades National Park in Florida, with the alligator's tail protruding from the snake's burst midsection.

So it seems that you can only burst – in real life or on film – if you are a python.

Chilli Sauce Score: ♪♪♪♪

MEMENTO

(2000, Dir. Christopher Nolan)

The bit where Guy Pearce realises he can't make new memories

So far we've see humans becoming magnetized, cutting their skin off and gobbling so much that they go splat. But could anything be worse than the living nightmare which Guy Pearce inhabits in this masterful reverse-chronology thriller: that of being unable to… um… what was it…? Pearce plays Leonard Shelby, who, having been attacked and suffered a bang to the head, develops the (genuine) condition anterograde amnesia, otherwise known as short-term memory loss. But can a person really be utterly unable to create and store new memories? And if so, what kind of life is that?

Amnesia has been used as a plot device in many films, but rarely realistically. How many comedies have you seen where a character gets hit on the head, forgets who and where they are, and only regains their memory after receiving another knock to the noggin? Do you think a second injury to an already injured brain works in real life? Do I even need to ask? By contrast, *Memento*'s depiction of anterograde amnesia has been given a relatively clean bill of health by the medical profession. Just as with real sufferers, Leonard is unable to create memories of facts and recent experiences – although unlike most he resorts to tattooing his body with details that he wants to remember. He also isn't affected by retrograde (past) amnesia. Leonard knows that he is Leonard.

Real-life memory has been described as a series of "bins". In effect, Leonard has damaged his short-term memory bin, which stores new experiences for minutes to hours before they are consolidated and placed in long-term storage. There is another bin called the working memory bin, which holds experiences for a second or two and enables people to think logically, speak coherently and hold conversations. As with other anterograde amnesiacs, Leonard's working memory bin remains in working order. So *Memento* is close to reality. The trouble is that nobody is quite sure what real memory is or how it works. Bins are one hypothesis, yet the precise mechanism for storing memories is not understood.

The most famous studies undertaken, and on which the film is seemingly based, were on a patient called Henry Molaison who, in 1953, developed severe anterograde amnesia after neurosurgery to control his epilepsy. Henry could remember events before the operation but from then on he was unable to form new memories. He believed he was meeting every person for the first time: his carers had to reintroduce themselves at the start of every session. Most poignantly, after his mother died, every time he heard about her passing it was as if he hadn't known.

Henry's fragmented existence is cleverly reflected in the backwards structure of *Memento*. Yet all is not quite right. Leonard acquired his anterograde amnesia through physical assault whereas most people develop the condition because of severe epilepsy, a stroke, or the interruption of the brain's oxygen supply due to near-drowning or strangulation. Similarly, Leonard remembers the attack when he was injured, which is unusual for anyone suffering head trauma that leads to some kind of amnesia. Finally – and weirdly – Leonard doesn't think he has amnesia. "I don't have amnesia," he says. "I know who I am. I just can't form new memories." That, Leonard, is anterograde amnesia. So you do have amnesia, just not the retrograde type you're thinking of.

But who can blame him for forgetting the difference?

Chilli Sauce Score:

THE NAME OF THE ROSE

(1986, Dir. Jean-Jacques Annaud)

The bit where Salvatore the hunchback speaks in tongues

 From Hellboy and Vincent in *Beauty and the Beast* to a brutish prisoner in a Stella beer commercial, Ron Perlman has carved out a niche looking rough on film. A great actor with an extraordinary face, Perlman's unsightly breakthrough came when he played the misshapen, boil-coated, dentally-challenged Salvatore in the film version of Umberto Eco's mediaeval murder mystery. In a stunning performance, Perlman spends much of the film talking in a devilish mix of Italian, French, English and Latin. He seems to be speaking in tongues.

"Penitenziagite! Watch out for the draco who cometh in futurum to gnaw on your anima! La mort e supremos! You contemplata me apocalypsum, eh? Là bas! Nous avons il diabolo! Ugly cum Salvatore, eh? My little brother! Penitenziagite!" As William of Baskerville, the Franciscan friar-cum-super sleuth played by Sean Connery, says of Salvatore, "He speaks in all languages – and none."

"Macaronic" is the term used for text spoken or written in a mixture of languages. The word is thought to have originated in 14th-century Padua, and derives from the well-known pasta dish. Another term is "code-switching" which generally refers to a combination of languages used in spoken conversation, often by multilingual communities. However, both macaronic language and code-switching tend to be used intentionally and rationally, to emphasize or minimize social or cultural differences. Salvatore's babblings are far more instinctive, illogical, mystical...

So is the hunchback practising glossolalia: "speaking in

tongues"? With origins in both Old and New Testaments, this fluent, rhythmic, language-like vocalization that many religious devotees seem driven or inspired to utter is seen by some to be a sign of spiritual possession, by others a sign of madness or play-acting. In 2006, researchers at the University of Pennsylvania took brain images of five female churchgoers while they spoke in tongues. They found that the subjects' frontal lobes — the thinking part of the brain where you control what you do — were relatively quiet, as were the language areas. Yet, the regions controlling self-consciousness were active.

So the subjects weren't in a trance, but the researchers still couldn't tell which part of the brain was causing the glossolalia. However, the women themselves were willing to offer their own diagnosis. They said that God was talking through them. Interestingly, one of the researchers was a born-again Christian who also believed that she could speak in tongues. "You're aware of your surroundings," she said. "You're not really out of control. But you have no control over what's happening. You're just flowing. You're in a realm of peace and comfort, and it's a fantastic feeling."

So does the hectic, heretic hunchback speak in tongues, and is glossolalia bona fide spiritual communication? Possibly. But, in truth, God alone knows.

Chilli Sauce Score: ♪♪♪

THE WORLD IS NOT ENOUGH

(1999, Dir. Michael Apted)

The bit where Renard can't feel pain

 Cinema audiences may have wished they couldn't either, as they watched Denise Richards' excruciating turn as Dr Christmas Jones in Pierce Brosnan's third outing as Bond. Admittedly there's no law stating that nuclear physicists can't be young, female and attractive, though believability is stretched almost as much as Richards' tight vest and micro-shorts. This time Bond has to foil a plan involving nuclear meltdown and control of the oil market, and comes up against Robert Carlyle's Renard, a KGB agent turned terrorist who is unable to feel pain. But is this painfully far from reality?

The reason given for Renard's analgesia is a bullet which is working its way through his brain. On its way, the bullet has eliminated Renard's senses of taste, smell and feeling, and this last deficit enables the terrorist to push his body past normal physical limits.

So how does pain go about its nasty work?

Pain receptors in the body are stimulated by chemicals released by damaged cells. The receptors then transmit signals via sensory nerves to the spinal cord, where the signals are processed in an area called the dorsal horn. Pain signals are then sent up the spinal cord to the thalamus, located at the base of the brain. Simultaneously, messages are sent from the spinal cord via motor nerves to the arm muscles, which contract quickly in an automatic reflex.

Further processing takes place in the thalamus, with signals being sent to areas controlling blood pressure, heart rate, breathing and emotions, as well as to the primary sensory cortex in the outer surface of the brain. With the emotional centres in the brain involved, it makes sense that our perception of pain depends in part on how we are feeling. Under normal conditions, the brain sends continuous signals down to the dorsal horn to keep the latter from sending too many signals upwards and causing sensory overload. When emotions like anger, fear or excitement are felt, even more of these jamming signals are sent to the dorsal horn, and this makes it still harder for the pain signals to break through to the brain. That's why soldiers often do not feel the pain from an injury until the heat of battle has subsided. Being happy can also help to block pain, while negative emotions like anxiety and depression reduce the signals descending from the brain, making it easier for pain signals to travel upwards.

Because pain has a strong psychological element, scientists and doctors have begun to find ways of influencing patients' emotions and environments in order to lessen the pain. For example, some burn patients in the US are encouraged to play a virtual reality computer game called SnowWorld in order to distract them from their injuries. The game involves throwing snowballs at snowmen, igloos, mammoths and penguins, and several patients have reported feeling almost no pain when they played the game whilst undergoing treatment for their burns.

You don't have to be injured to experience the effects of pain, as a team from University College London discovered. During tests involving couples in relationships, they found that watching the pain suffered by a partner (when stimulation was applied to their hand) was enough to trigger activity in some of the pain centres of the observing partner's brain. (How often have you thought "Ouch! I *felt* that"?)

Some painkilling drugs work in the same way as "positive" emotions by making the pain-blocking signals stronger. Other methods of pain suppression include rubbing an injured area or applying heat. These methods stimulate vibration receptors, which send signals to the dorsal horn and, again, block pain signals to the brain.

Or, like Renard, you can simply be unable to experience pain. In real life, this is a genetic rather than a shot-in-the-head condition. And it's not the blessing you might have imagined. Take a boy from Yorkshire, who is only the 33rd person ever to be diagnosed with what is known as congential analgesia. The boy's parents first noticed that something was different when their son was nine months old and he took a hot chip from his father's plate and blistered three fingers – without showing any signs of pain. Since then, he has run around after fracturing his heel bone and been similarly unaffected after pulling out a tooth. But with no pain signals to tell the toddler when he has been harmed, his parents need to keep a constant watch.

Also afflicted by congential analgesia are Steven Pete from the US and Paul Waters from the UK, who have jointly set up a website to educate people about their condition. Growing up, both Steven and Paul had to wear socks on their hands, goggles and helmets to protect themselves. Even so, burnt skin and broken legs were common. Another fascinating insight that Steven and Paul give is that having congenital analgesia does not in any way make them unfeeling. So, if one of them were to be cut by a knife, they would feel the blade slicing through their skin but without the pain. And they feel emotional pain in the same way as everyone else.

Something that could not be said for Renard.

Chilli Sauce Score: ♪♪

CITIZEN KANE

(1941, Dir. Orson Welles)

The bit where Charles Foster Kane wiggles his ears

Orson Welles co-wrote, produced, directed and starred in this monumental character-study of the fictional Charles Foster Kane, a thinly-veiled portrayal of the life of newspaper magnate William Randolph Hearst. *Citizen Kane* is often considered the most accomplished film ever made. And for good reason. Technically innovative and inventively structured, it's a *tour-de-force* of cinema. And not only did Welles achieve all this at only twenty-five years old; he also appears on screen wiggling both his ears at the same time.

According to Kane, this was a trick taught to him by the future President of Venezuela and took two years to master. But can people really wiggle their ears, and can it be learned? Charles Darwin certainly thought so and provides pretty much the perfect answer in *The Descent of Man*: "The extrinsic muscles which serve to move the external ear, and the intrinsic muscles which move the different parts, are in a rudimentary condition in man, and they all belong to the system of the *panniculus*; they are also variable in development, or at least in function. I have seen one man who could draw the whole ear forwards; other men can draw it upwards; another who could draw it backwards; and from what one of these persons told me, it is probable that most of us, by often touching our ears, and thus directing our attention towards them, could recover some power of movement by repeated trials. The power of erecting and directing the shell of the ears to the various points of the compass, is no doubt of the highest service to many animals, as they thus perceive the direction of danger."

What more can be added? Well, the rudimentary muscles in the ear are called vestigial structures, which means they have

lost all or most of their original function through evolution. Vestigial they may be, but ear muscles can still be used to set world records, as documented by that arbiter of the limits of human endeavour and sporting prowess, the RecordSetter website (www.recordsetter.com). RecordSetter regulations state, "In documenting ear wiggling world record attempts, we count a wiggle as a movement of the ears from their resting place to a visibly displaced position and back again. Ears must be wiggled in tandem for an attempt to be recognized." And in 2009, one Ross Martin set an impressive record of 79 wiggles in 30 seconds.

Yes, the skill of ear wiggling is a reality, and it can be learned, practiced and honed to world-beating levels. So Charles Foster Kane was right when he said "I don't think there's one word that can describe a man's life."

In fact, it takes two: ear wiggler.

Chilli Sauce Score: 𝅘𝅥

OBJECTS

"I love rumors! Facts can be so misleading, where rumors, true or false, are often revealing."

Inglourious Basterds

THE KING'S SPEECH

(2010, Dir. Tom Hooper)

The bit where King Edward's chair is covered in graffiti

This film concerns a speech therapist's attempts to cure a man of his stutter. Not the most exciting premise in cinema history. But throw in a bit of royalty, a dash of family conflict, the outbreak of World War II and top-drawer performances from Colin Firth and Geoffrey Rush, and you have an entertaining and moving Oscar-winner on your hands. Rush plays Lionel Logue, tasked with helping Firth's King George VI overcome his speech impediment. Logue's methods are as nonconformist as they are ultimately successful, and include lounging around on King Edward's chair in Westminster Abbey. But have people (as Logue says) really carved their names all over the 700-year-old Coronation Chair?

First, let's make one thing clear. We're talking about the chair made for Edward I to enclose the Stone of Scone, which he had brought from Scotland to Westminster Abbey in 1296. Not about the very different chair commissioned 600 years later by his successor, King Edward VII – one that would take his weight whilst having sex in a Parisian brothel called Le Chabanais. This elaborate chair, complete with two tiers of seat and stirrups, allowed the rotund Edward to fornicate with two women at the same time without having a coronary. No wonder the Prince, when he became king, was nicknamed Edward the Carresser.

Back to Edward I's chair. The two-metre tall, Gothic-style chair built was carved from oak and was painted by one Master Walter, who decorated it with birds, animals and foliage. The figure of Edward the Confessor with his feet resting on a lion was painted on the back of the chair. Four gilded lions were added to the base in the 1500s. The Stone of Scone was originally enclosed in a space

under the chair's seat and was there for the coronation of every subsequent English king and queen except for Edwards V and VIII (who were not officially crowned) and Mary II (who, because she was crowned alongside her husband William III, had to make do with a replica).

King Edward's chair is currently undergoing restoration, for it is indeed covered in graffiti (Italian for 'little scratches'). Much of the wood has been carved with names and initials, many of which belong to those perennial mischief-makers: schoolboys. 18th and 19th-century pupils from Westminster School seem to have been the main culprits, including one P. Abbott who inscribed on the ancient oak that he had 'slept in this chair 5, 6 July 1800'.

There is one other (more recent) piece of graffiti worth mentioning. On Christmas Day 1950, the Stone of Scone was stolen by Scottish Nationalists. It was recovered four months later. But the Scots had made their point and left their mark: for a new carving had appeared on King Edward's chair. It reads 'J.F.S.' and it is believed to stand for Justice For Scotland. And in 1996, the British Government agreed to return the stone to Scotland, so long as it could still be used for coronations. The Stone of Scone can now be seen in Edinburgh Castle.

Here today, Scone tomorrow.

Chilli Sauce Score:)

MODERN TIMES

(1936, Dir. Charlie Chaplin)

The bit where Charlie Chaplin lights a match on the seat of his trousers

A mental breakdown, a Communist demonstration, cocaine abuse, a jailbreak, theft, car crash, assault on a police officer. Welcome to one of the most cherished of all Chaplin's silent films. Starring his best-loved character the Tramp, *Modern Times* provides a memorable commentary on the unstoppable progress of industrialization exemplified by the iconic scene of a frenetic Chaplin trying to keep up with a factory production line. He also finds time to light a match on his trousers. But does that match reality?

Striking a match on the trouser zip is an old schoolboy favourite. But we don't see Chaplin fishing for his flies. It's from the seat of his pants that he summons fire.

As with many inventions, the earliest matches may well have come from China, where people coated sticks with sulphur to help with lighting fires. However, it wasn't until 1826 that a British chemist called John Walker invented friction matches when he discovered that a mixture of antimony(III) sulphide, potassium chlorate, gum and starch would catch fire when struck against a surface. Walker's invention was patented by one Samuel Jones, who sold the matches as "lucifers" – in some countries including the Netherlands they're still known as such. The diabolical name was appropriate: they were hellishly volatile, igniting spontaneously and throwing sparks over a wide area. Chaplin would certainly have been able to light these matches on his trousers, though he may never have been able to sit down again.

Lucifers also reeked. To counter this, Frenchman Charles Sauria added white phosphorus in 1830. Unfortunately, those who made

these matches often developed a condition called "phossy jaw" and there was enough white phosphorus in one pack to kill a person. (Another contemporary option was to dispense with matches altogether and use a loco-foco, a self-igniting cigar patented in New York in 1834. The loco-foco did not catch on as readily as it caught fire.) In response to the danger of white phosphorous, safety matches were developed in the 1840s by Swede Gustaf Erik Pasch and then improved by Johan Edvard Lundström. Safety matches were so called because the combustible ingredients were split between the end of a paraffin-impregnated splint and a special striking surface, which contained red rather than white phosphorus.

The rest of the 19th century saw improvements to the chemical compounds used in matches, as well as the development of "strike anywhere" matches. Because their tips contain the phosphorus, these will ignite when struck, if not anywhere, then at any rate against a rough surface. Today, strike-anywhere matches are banned in certain places, e.g. in Minnesota (where it's also illegal to sleep naked). Elsewhere, they are produced with different levels of phosphorus so that they can be struck on a wide range of surfaces from wood and rocks to teeth.

And, almost certainly, Charlie Chaplin's pants.

Chilli Sauce Score: 𝄪

A CONNECTICUT YANKEE IN KING ARTHUR'S COURT

(1949, Dir. Tay Garnett)

The bit where a telescope is used in the year 528 AD

In this whimsical adaptation of a Mark Twain novel, Bing Crosby plays Hank Martin, a mechanic who receives a bang on the head and wakes to find himself in the time of King Arthur (this outcome is *definitely* not scientifically attested). Cue a succession of modern inventions that Crosby uses to mystify and impress the king and his court. But one object with which the England of the early sixth century seems to be already familiar is the telescope. Surely it was invented much later than 528 AD?

In the film, it is Merlin the sorcerer who uses a telescope. But it is generally accepted that a Dutch spectacle maker, Hans Lippershey invented the telescope using converging and diverging lenses in 1608 – over a millennium after the film was set. A year later, Galileo Galilei built his own model, pointed it at the sky and began to make astronomical discoveries, such as the four moons orbiting Jupiter.

But the origin of the lens itself is much less clear. It was long supposed that glass lenses were not invented until the 13th century when Roger Bacon, rather wonderfully nicknamed 'Doctor Mirabilis', used part of a solid glass sphere as a magnifying glass. However, as early as the 11th and 12th centuries, monks used glass spheres cut in half when illuminating their manuscripts. As these 'reading stones' were experimented with, it was discovered that shallower lenses magnified more effectively.

Yet Ibn al-Haytham – who was born circa 965 in Basra (in what is now Iraq) and is now referred to as the father of modern optics

– had already published his *Book of Optics* over a century earlier. His work, which contains a description of the magnification produced by lenses, was subsequently translated into Latin and became accessible to European scholars (monks included).

Even that may not have been the start of it. In 1850, an archaeologist called John Layard, excavating at the palace of Nimrud (also in modern-day Iraq), discovered what appeared to be a rock crystal lens. That would put the invention of lenses back three thousand years, to the time of the ancient Assyrians. Another object thought to be an ancient lens, dating from the 5th century B.C., was found in a cave on Mount Ida on Crete.

Whenever the lens was invented, it remains extremely unlikely that a magician in the employ of King Arthur discovered that, by combining concave and convex lenses, he could make distant objects appear much closer, some one thousand years before the telescope's accepted date of invention. And that's without taking into account that there was no single historical figure called Merlin. And perhaps even no Arthur and no court at Camelot.

But let's not go *there*.

Chilli Sauce Score: ♪ ♪ ♪ ♪ ♪

MISSION: IMPOSSIBLE

(1996, Dir. Brian De Palma)

The bit where Tom uses explosive chewing gum

"Red light! Green light!" Forget Juicy Fruit and Hubba Bubba, we're talking gum with real gumption. One of a boxful of hi-tech tricks in this homage to the TV series, Tom's chewie not only helps him destroy a vast fish tank but also brings down a helicopter... in the Channel Tunnel.

From an impossible mission to an imbecilic one: in 2009, a chemistry student in the northern Ukrainian city of Konotop was found dead with his jaw blown off by what was believed to be exploding chewing gum. The 25-year-old had been studying at Kiev Polytechnic Institute and was working at his computer late one night when, according to an aide to the city's police chief, "a loud pop was heard from the student's room. When his relatives entered the room, they saw that the lower part of the young man's face had been blown off."

An examination of the student's room yielded some chewed-up gum covered in an unidentified substance. Further investigation showed that the student was partial to dipping his gum in citric acid, presumably because chewing Ukranian gum is a bit like masticating a condom. Along with the citric acid packets in the room, police found a substance of near-identical appearance, believed to be some kind of explosive chemical. It seems that the student confused the packets, dipped his gum in the explosive substance, popped it in his mouth and pop went the weasel.

Chilli Sauce Score: ⟩⟩⟩

INGLOURIOUS BASTERDS

(2009, Dir. Quentin Tarantino)

The bit where burning nitrate film stock kills a cinema full of Nazis

Only Tarantino could be so bold, making a World War II film in the style of a spaghetti western and rewriting history by ending the war in 1944. Brad Pitt leads a team of Jewish-American soldiers, the Basterds, as they go about scalping the German army one by one. Austrian Christoph Waltz stole the show and an Academy Award for his unforgettable turn as Colonel Hans Landa. And Hitler and the Nazi High Command get an uncomfortably warm reception at a French cinema.

The nitrate film stock in the cinema is piled up behind the screen and then ignited, causing fire to rampage through the building. And it really is that flammable. Nitrate film was used for most of the period from the mid-1890s to the 1950s and was very good at its job, providing a hard-wearing medium for carrying moving images. However, being closely related to gun cotton, cellulose nitrate does burn viciously. To make matters worse, nitrate contains its own oxygen, meaning it is pretty much impossible to extinguish. The film will continue to burn underwater and also generates large quantities of toxic fumes. No wonder that today old nitrate film is stored in purpose-built, secure archive facilities. The Imperial War Museum's Film and Video Archive separates its nitrate film into small quantities which it stores in separate cells to stop fire spreading. (When the IWM built new vaults for its archive, they deliberately burned one ton of film in a cell to ensure that its design was sound.) The British Film Institute takes a different, although equally cautious approach, hiding most of its nitrate stock in limestone quarries in Warwickshire.

Today's extreme caution is the product of a shocking number of fatalities caused by nitrate fires in cinemas. The sad list of accidents includes 125 deaths at the Bazar de la Charité Fair in Paris in 1897; over 250 deaths at the Flores Theatre in Acapulco in 1909; nearly 100 killed in Bologoye, Russia in 1911; over 100 deaths in Smyrna, Turkey in 1924; and 58 fatalities in Wielopole Skrzyńskie, Poland in 1955. But none is more heart-rending than two incidents that happened in cinemas in Montreal in 1927, and in Paisley, Scotland in 1929. In the first, 77 children died. In the second, 70 children.

Nitrate film really is dangerous. It's a tragedy that so many have lost their lives simply by going to the cinema, a place they had hoped would bring them wonder and enjoyment.

Chilli Sauce Score: ⌡

THE EARLY BIRD

(1965, Dir. Robert Asher)

The bit where Norman Wisdom is thrown around in the air by a fire hose

This has to be the archetypal Norman Wisdom film (even though it's his first one shot in colour) and a fitting tribute to his memory. Wisdom is back as the (often literally) down-to-earth Norman Pitkin, who works for Grimsdale's Dairy as a milkman. Cue the usual mayhem with a wayward lawnmower, a sick horse, a fake vicar, a crazy game of golf and the moment when Pitkin assumes the role of fire chief and is lifted into the air by a fire hose, soaking everyone in sight. But is this false wisdom?

Today's fire engines are pretty serious bits of kit, even if many of them seem to be called Dennis. The standard engines go by the even more boring name of Water Tender Ladder Rescue. They hold around 1800 litres of water and have 2 fixed hose reels, plus a hose jet for delivering a more powerful stream of water. The working pressure for a fire hose (also called a branch) ranges between 8 and 20 bar or 100 and 300 psi (for comparison, the air in a car's tyres is pressurized to around 32 psi).

So what stops firefighters doing a Pitkin? Training. The force of the water shooting out of the hose is known as the jet reaction and there have been instances on public open days of its knocking people off their feet or pinning them against walls, if not exactly lifting them into the air. (This was in the days before the spoilsports from Health and Safety stopped the fun.)

In real emergencies, firefighters usually have a branch man (or woman) directing the hose, with a second firefighter behind to assist in taking the strain. If a hose does break free, the pressure is decreased to bring it back under control, since there's a risk of

serious injury if it whips someone in the face. It's not all about the pressure, though. After all, your garden hose releases water at high pressure yet it doesn't usually attack you like a crazed anaconda. The volume of water is equally crucial. The bigger the diameter of the hose, the more water it discharges and the more difficult it can be to control even at low pressure.

In the end, the reason why Norman Wisdom was riding on air was that he had a large hose.

Chilli Sauce Score: ♪♪♪

NATIONAL LAMPOON'S CHRISTMAS VACATION

(1989, Dir. Jeremiah S. Chechik)

The bit where Clark Griswold lights up his home with 25,000 Christmas lights

"Yule crack up!" So goes the tagline, and whilst that can't be said of all the *Vacation* film series, *Christmas Vacation* contains its fair share of festive frivolity. Which is just as well, since these days it's on TV every Christmas.

Clark Griswold (Chevy Chase) covers his house with thousands of lights, as a result of which the town suffers a blackout, an extra nuclear power station has to be fired up and Aunt Bethany asks, "Is your house on fire, Clark?" Griswold reckons he has 250 strands of lights, with 100 bulbs per strand. But the bulbs he uses are the old-fashioned filament type, which need around 7 watts each. So for his 25,000 bulbs he'd require 175,000 watts of power, which is far more than can usually be delivered to a home. But instead of the town suffering a blackout, it would be Griswold's own pad that would see its circuit breakers trip… without special preparation, that is.

In fact, 25,000 bulbs are nothing compared to what some homes have to bear, albeit with the benefit of energy-saving LED lights. Take Alex Goodwin's house in Melksham, Wiltshire, which he decked with 115,000 lights in 2009. Or Dave Rezendes, a church deacon from Livermore in California, who has been lighting up his house for over 20 years. His finest moment came in 2003 with his design "North Pole Flight Training Centre", which required 230,000 lights. Building work on the light display began the weekend before Labor Day in August and the utility company had to install an industrial transformer on the street to deliver the 400 amps required. Apparently, the Rev. Rezendes sees his Christmas light displays as "a gift to the community". I'd like to know if his neighbours across the street feel the same way.

Or how about the aptly named Clot family from Miami? Their home completely disappeared in 2008 under 600,000 bulbs and 100 animated displays, with the Clots' electricity bill reaching an eye-watering $4,000 a month. However, the undoubted winners are the Fauchers from Delaware. 700,000 bulbs? 800,000? No, 1,000,000 bulbs illuminated the Faucher home, and half of the Eastern Seaboard.

So with a lot of planning and electrical expertise, Clark Griswold could well have covered his abode with 25,000 Christmas lights. But planning, expertise and Griswold don't really go together, do they?

Chilli Sauce Score: ♪♪

OCTOPUSSY

(1983, Dir. John Glen)

The bit where a goon crushes dice with his bare hands

Is it right that 007 should hide in a gorilla suit, disguise himself as a clown and swing through the trees whilst giving a Tarzan cry? It's just not Bond. But never mind; it's all good fun as Roger Moore uncovers an elaborate smuggling operation and a plot by a renegade Soviet general to start World War III.

At one point, while playing exiled Afghan prince Kamal Khan at backgammon, Bond exposes his opponent as a cheat, provoking Khan's burly henchman into crushing his master's loaded dice into dust. From Quint in *Jaws* crushing a beer can to Oddjob in *Goldfinger* mangling a golf ball, pulverizing whatever is closest to hand is an oft-used sign of movie manliness. But surely dice would be too hard?

Dice are the oldest gaming implements known to man, though their prehistoric origins seem to lie not in games but the divination of the future. Knucklebones or the anklebones of sheep formed the first dice; the Arabic word for knucklebone is the same as the word for dice, and in Arab countries even today dice are sometimes referred to as bones. Over the centuries dice have also been made from pebbles, seeds, shells and teeth. Excavations in Egypt have uncovered stone dice from 2000 B.C. that look very similar to their modern-day descendants. And dice have been discovered among the remains of virtually every culture, from Ancient China to the Inuit.

The Greeks and Romans liked their dice made from bone, ivory and occasionally semi-precious stones. Etruscan dice dating from around 900 B.C. found near Rome are similar to today's dice in that their opposing faces always add up to seven. Roman

soldiers used dice to cast lots for Christ's robe in the Bible and Julius Caesar declared that "Jacta alea est" – the die is cast – when crossing the Rubicon.

Students of human nature will not be surprised to learn that among these ancient artefacts are plentiful and widespread examples of loaded dice. Archaeologists have discovered dice that have been weighted in favour of landing on a particular side in Viking graves, the tombs of Ancient Egyptians and buried in the ash of Pompeii. But weighting is not the only way to fix the dice to improve your chances. "Shapes" are dice that have been shaved down on one side, leaving them very slightly brick-shaped and so more likely to land on one of their longer sides. Meanwhile, "tops" and "bottoms" are dice with incorrectly numbered faces which take advantage of the fact that only three faces of a die can be seen at any one time. So one die might have three, four, and five each repeated on two of its faces whilst the other might have pairs of one, five, and six – the result being that the two dice could never combine for a throw totaling seven. To combat cheating, casinos ensure their dice are made to exact specifications. Each die is sawn from cellulose acetate rods to form a perfect cube to within one five-thousandth of an inch. Then each spot is drilled to be precisely seventeen-thousandths of an inch deep before being filled with paint weighing exactly the same as the acetate that was removed.

But all this is by way of digression. If you discovered that someone was cheating (or if you wanted to dispose of the evidence of your own sharp practices), would you be able to crush dice to dust in your bare hands?

Grip and crushing feats have long been a staple of strongman (and woman) displays, from bending coins and breaking nails to tearing books and even crushing potatoes. The British Grip Championships were established in 1991, and today hand strength is big business with all sorts of contraptions being marketed as helping to improve your grip. One of the most famous

is the Captains of Crush torsion-spring hand gripper, which has become an internationally-recognised measure of hand strength. There are four main grades of gripper in the Captains of Crush range, with the No.4 model being the hardest to close. To date, only five men have ever managed to muster up the 365 pounds of pressure required to bring the No.4 gripper's handles together. But would that be enough pressure to turn dice into dust? With today's dice being made from solid cellulose acetate, the answer is – of course – no.

And that's something we'll just have to get to grips with.

Chilli Sauce Score:)))))

CHARADE

(1963, Dir. Stanley Donen)

The bit where Cary Grant appears cleverer when wearing glasses

That's not a mistake: Stanley Donen directed this sixties classic, not Alfred Hitchcock. Yet with its masterful blend of thrills, comedy and romance, it's no wonder many people believe it to be the work of Hitch. Cary Grant goes under four different names as he helps and hinders Audrey Hepburn to find out why her husband was murdered. At one point Grant puts on reading-glasses. But is he trying to appear more intelligent than he really is? Is it just a charade?

No, as it turns out when Hepburn tries on the glasses. "You need them," she says. Yet spectacles and stereotypes do go hand-in-hand on film, from the Nazi torturer's rimless specs to the shady type in shades. Perhaps the most common cliché of all is the geek squinting behind his or her spectacles. But what's the real deal with clever people wearing glasses?

The most common and obvious answer is that intelligent people wear glasses because they've strained their eyes by reading too many books. This seems to have at least a possible basis in fact, since focusing on things close-up can strain the cillary muscles that control the lenses in your eyes. When you look at something close-to, the lenses are made thicker by the cillary muscles; do this a lot and the cillary muscles lose their ability to revert back to normal, keeping the lenses thicker and making it harder to see things far away. Hence bookworms might come to require glasses.

Alternatively perhaps it's that children who wear glasses get bullied and teased, and so end up spending more time in their own company with books and the internet. Chicken or egg?

Enough guesswork; now for some real science. In 2008, the

University of Melbourne's Centre for Eye Research Australia conducted a study to find if there are any personality traits linked to short-sightedness. During the study, the glasses-wearing subjects were evaluated according to five characteristics: extroversion, conscientiousness, openness, agreeableness and neuroticism. It turned out that there was a strong link between short-sightedness and openness, a personality trait which correlates with having a wide range of interests and being intelligent.

There is one other link between clever people and glasses – and that's when the glasses themselves are intelligent. Japanese scientists (who else?) have invented a pair of "smart goggles" that can help people remember where they left their keys, phone, wallet, etc., as well as being able to identify unfamiliar faces and plants. The specs contain a camera that films everything the wearer looks at. The images are transmitted to a small computer, worn as a backpack, that can recognise objects and people, the locations or names of which are displayed on a small screen in front of the right lens.

So it seems that wearing glasses can actually make you more intelligent. Isn't that clever?

Chilli Sauce Score: ♪♪

THE ILLUSIONIST

(2006, Dir. Neil Burger)

The bit where Edward Norton summons a ghost on stage

 Here's another film in which little is what it seems. This time Edward Norton is the mysterious leading man, a magician in turn-of-the-twentieth-century Vienna. Writer and director Neil Burger references many illusions from what many consider the golden age of magic. Sudden vanishings, impossibly heavy swords and miraculous orange trees all made appearances (or disappearances) on the 19th-century stage. But what about making an actual (so to speak) ghost appear? Was the illusion possible?

Jessica Biel is the ghost in question. She plays Sophie, the Duchess von Teschen, the illusionist's childhood sweetheart but betrothed to the ruthless Crown Prince Leopold. The potty Prince apparently murders Sophie. However, the lovelorn magician soon unveils a new illusion in which he sits on a dark stage and summons the glowing and translucent apparition of his dead beloved.

This trick is actually known as Pepper's Ghost, named after Professor John Henry Pepper, a lecturer on science at the Royal Polytechnic Institution in Victorian London. Pepper had refined the illusion from an optical principle discovered by a civil engineer called Henry Dirks. The principle is simple. Look through a window at night and you see your ghostly reflection looking back at you. Your face is strangely transparent, floating at a distance that seems to be neither here nor there. What you are seeing is Pepper's Ghost.

What Dirks, and then Pepper, realised was that this phenomenon could be used in the theatre. A large, spotlessly clean pane of glass was placed on stage between the actors and the audience (before the audience took their seats so as to keep it secret) and was angled down so that it faced into the orchestra pit. The pit was draped in black fabric and, also unseen by the audience, the actor playing the ghost was put in the pit and tilted on a board so that he or she directly faced the pane of glass. A bright light in the pit shone onto the actor causing their transparent, ghostly reflection to appear in the glass. With careful choreography, the actors on stage could interact with the apparition, seeming to hold its hand (as in *The Illusionist*) or even to act out a swordfight. If the light was dimmed and turned off in the pit, the ghost would dissolve into thin air.

So that's how to summon a ghost on stage. Does that means *The Illusionist* is true to life? Not quite. For when the film was set, single sheets of glass were only available in sizes up to nine by fifteen feet. As a result, Pepper's Ghost was only really suitable for very small theatres: the theatre in the film is way too big. Also, the glass across the stage meant that the actors behind it couldn't be heard properly by the audience, so the ghost was only used in mimed plays. Finally, in the film, Paul Giamatti's Chief Inspector rushes onto stage at the end of the illusion.

If there'd been a large sheet of glass in his way he'd certainly have known about it.

Chilli Sauce Score: 🌶🌶🌶

GOLDFINGER

(1964, Dir. Guy Hamilton)

The bit where Oddjob decapitates a statue with his bowler hat

 "Do you expect me to talk?"

"No, Mr Bond. I expect you to die."

A great line from a great Bond film, one that swaggers from one iconic moment to the next: white dinner jacket, gold paint, silver DB5, red laser. And black bowler hat. Auric Goldfinger's super-strong sidekick Oddjob is a man of few words (none, in fact). But when you've got a razor-sharp, steel-edged bowler, it's easier to let your hat do the talking.

The hard-crowned bowler was designed in 1850 by James Lock and Co. of 6 St James's Street, London. The first hats were made for the Hon. Edward Coke, to give his gamekeepers protection from low-hanging branches and low-bred poachers as they patrolled Sir William's land on horseback. The hats were actually produced by hatters Bowler Brothers, whose name was adopted for the new style (no doubt partly due to its bowl shape).

In the United States, the bowler was known as the derby: it was popular with racegoers. And street gangs. The cities of mid-nineteenth century America saw a proliferation of gangs. There were the Bowery Boys, the Chichesters and the Dead Rabbits Gang, who specialised in mugging, pickpocketing and robbery, and went around with a dead bunny on a spear. One gang even had a list of their services printed up: "Punching - $2. Both Eyes Blackened - $4. Nose & Jaw Broken - $10. Jacked Out [knocked out with a blackjack] - $15. Ear Chawed Off - $15. Leg Or Arm Broken - $19. Shot in The Leg - $25. Stab - $25. Doing the Job [murder] $100 and up."

Then there were the splendidly titled Plug Uglies. The gang, who required that all their members were of Irish descent and over six feet tall, got their name from the plug – a.k.a. bowler – hats they wore (which may have inspired Stanley Kubrick to dress the droogs with bowlers in *A Clockwork Orange*). And the Plug Uglies certainly seem to have needed the protection. The gang operated in Baltimore between 1853 and 1860, mainly as the enforcing arm of the equally-splendidly-named 'Know Nothing' anti-immigrant political movement. Reports of elections in Baltimore describe the Plug Uglies threatening voters. One account from 1856 even talks of brass cannon being used. Away from election time, the Plug Uglies were engaged in the day-to-day activities of street crime, shootings and assassinations. It is surely possible that, as well as wearing their reinforced bowlers for their own safety, gang members in a fix might have removed their headgear in order to use it as a weapon.

So in the wrong hands, bowler hats could indeed be dangerous. Although the likelihood of one being able to decapitate a stone statue – even when edged with steel and thrown by Harold Sakata, who, in addition from playing Oddjob won a weightlifting silver medal at the 1948 London Olympics – is very low indeed.

Prove me wrong, and I'll eat my hat.

Chilli Sauce Score:))))

DUCK SOUP

(1933. Dir, Leo McCarey)

The bit where Harpo pretends to be Groucho's reflection

There's no accounting for taste. No, not of the soup, but of the moviegoers and critics who gave this Marx Brothers comedy a distinctly lukewarm reception. The film is a classic, containing some of the brothers' most outrageous lines ("I got a good mind to join a club and beat you over the head with it") and hilarious stunts. The most famous of which is the mirror scene.

Groucho – playing Rufus T. Firefly, dressed in a nightgown and cap with trademark black 'tache and cigar – peers through the space left by a broken mirror at Harpo, dressed exactly the same, pretending to be Firefly's reflection. Firefly tries to catch Pinky out through a series of spontaneous actions, but it's not until Chico arrives on the scene that the illusion is broken. Pure farce, brilliantly choreographed. But does the scene stand up to the principles of optical science?

Modern mirrors are made by spraying a thin layer of silver or aluminum onto the back of a sheet of glass. Photons of incoming light energy travel through the glass and are absorbed by the silver or aluminium atoms. This makes the atoms unstable, so they try to get rid of the extra energy by emitting more photons. This is reflection. According to the law of reflection, the light's angle of incidence when it hits the mirror is always equal to the angle of reflection when it bounces off. You probably knew that, and that a mirror reverses things – your real right hand becomes your reflection's left. But have you ever wondered, if left becomes right, why up doesn't also become down and vice versa?

It's because mirrors don't turn left into right at all, it just looks that way for roughly symmetrical things, like people. Hold a

non-symmetrical mug up to a mirror and its handle will still be pointing to the same side. Left is still left, right is still right, up is still up... What you perceive in a mirror is not what's really there but what you think is there, based on how you think the image is being created. What mirrors really do is turn front into back. Imagine if someone had reached through the back of your head, grabbed the tip of your nose and pulled it back through your head, along with the rest of you, so that you're facing the other way. (Don't try this at home.) Alternatively, and almost as messily, imagine being covered head-to-toe in paint and then pressing up against a large piece of paper. Everything's still on the same side, it's just that the front of the printed image is now facing you. That's what your mirror image really is: a light-print of you.

Mirrors play strange psychological tricks on us humans, mainly because we can't get our heads around their rules. Which makes it even more remarkable that those zany Marx boys did indeed manage to reflect the optical principles of mirrors so accurately.

And that's why the mirror scene is such a smash hit.

Chilli Sauce Score: ♪

BURIED

(2010, Dir. Rodrigo Cortés)

The bit where a coffin contains enough oxygen to last 90 minutes

The film opens on a US contractor in Iraq (played by Ryan Reynolds), who wakes up to find himself buried alive in a wooden coffin. He has a mobile phone, a pen, a torch, a lighter, a knife, a hipflask and a couple of glowsticks to keep him company. It transpires that his captors want a large ransom to release him. The camera stays with Reynolds in the coffin. And after a while you think, 'The film's going to cut away to the outside world soon.' But it doesn't. Not for one second in its whole ninety-or-so minutes. It's a testament to Reynolds' performance and in particular Cortés' direction that *Buried* never gets boring. In fact, it's a taut and (it goes without saying) claustrophobic affair throughout.

But, along with his actor, did Cortés also bury the truth of how long a person would be able to breathe in a sealed coffin?

It doesn't spoil the film to say that a lack of oxygen isn't a deciding factor in Reynolds' fate, and that Reynolds stays alive for the full hour-and-a-half running time. (Even given the most brilliant director, staring at a dead body in a coffin might not make great cinema.) But in reality, would the oxygen have run out much sooner?

First, the experienceof being buried alive isn't confined to the movies. Neither is it always thanks to the evil ways of wicked criminals. In days gone by medical equipment – specifically the instruments used to detect signs of life – wasn't very reliable. And so history is littered with cases of unfortunate people who have suffered that most awful of fates: premature burial. Take Madam Blunden, who in 1896 was buried in the Blunden family vault,

which was situated under a boys' school in Basingstoke. It was reported that the day after the funeral the schoolboys heard a noise from the vault below. The vault and Madam Blunden's coffin were hurriedly opened – just in time for her take her final breath. The poor woman had also scratched her face and bitten her nails off in anguish and desperation.

A few years earlier in 1885, a young man called Jenkins from Asheville, North Carolina, supposedly succumbed to fever. His flesh was cold and clammy and he appeared to have no pulse. Tellingly however, rigor mortis didn't set in. Indeed it was remarked that he was 'as limber as a live man'. (Can you see where this is going?) Nevertheless Jenkins was buried. Some days later, it was decided to move his coffin to the family burial ground. In order to see whether Jenkins' corpse had decayed to the extent that a metal coffin would be required to transport him, his original coffin was opened. Jenkins was now face down, his hair had been pulled out and the inside of the coffin's lid and sides were covered in scratches.

Perhaps most disturbing of all is the story of pregnant Madame Bobin who contracted yellow fever on board a steamer from West Africa in 1901. She was transferred to a hospital but (apparently) died and was buried. However, a nurse later (a little too late, it must be said) stated that the deceased Madame's skin had not been cold and that the muscles in her abdomen had seemed to twitch occasionally. When the Madame's father heard this he had the coffin dug up and opened. He not only discovered that Madame Bobin had died from asphyxiation rather than yellow fever, but that her baby had been born and had died alongside its mother in the coffin.

And the cases above are the ones that were discovered and reported. Who knows how many people actually went to their graves when they were alive and kicking and clawing at the insides of their coffins? In fact, when the Les Innocents cemetery in Paris

was relocated to the suburbs, the number of remains found face down seems to suggest that being buried alive was very common indeed.

So it's not surprising then that during the 19th century a number of designs for 'safety coffins' were patented with the purpose of preventing, if not premature burial, then premature burial turning into premature death. The most popular was called Bateson's Belfry and was patented by an Englishman, George Bateson, in 1852. It comprised of an iron bell mounted above ground and a cord which ran down from the bell, through the soil and then through a hole drilled in the coffin lid. The other end of the cord was placed in the deceased individual's hand. Queen Victoria herself was impressed by the design and gave Bateson an award for 'services to dead people'. (Shouldn't that be services to *still living* people?) However, the expression 'saved by the bell' does not originate from Bateson's Belfry (as is commonly thought) but from boxing (as is also commonly thought).

Never ones to do things by halves, our American cousins came up with their own, more elaborate ways of preventing premature burial. Christian Eisenbrandt of Baltimore, for example, invented a coffin in 1843 which had a spring-loaded lid that would open should the corpse resume breathing before burial. And also in the nineteenth century, Dr Timothy Clark Smith of Vermont was buried in a special crypt which contained a breathing tube and a glass window set into the ground above.

But if you have failed to take these precautions, how much oxygen will your coffin contain? Depending of course how much room you take up, there'll be enough oxygen to breathe for, on average, up to two hours. However, there are ways to decrease (and increase) the rate of oxygen consumption. For example, should you find yourself trapped in a coffin it's best to take deep breaths and then hold them for as long as you can before exhaling. And, unlike Ryan Reynolds, you should try and refrain

from shouting as this leads to faster breathing and an increased heart rate. Similarly, avoid using a lighter (again like Ryan), as this will increase the rate of oxygen consumption and decrease your life expectancy accordingly.

So the best way to survive being buried alive is to keep quiet and breathe deeply. But you still need to find a way out. And to do that it may well be best to follow the example of the author Roald Dahl who was buried with his snooker cues, some fine wine, chocolates, pencils… and a saw.

Chilli Sauce Score: ♪♪♪

NATURE

"We all see it. That don't make
it real."
Moby Dick

MAGNOLIA

(1999, Dir. Paul Thomas Anderson)

The bit where charred remains of a scuba diver are found in a forest fire

With nine connected storylines and a cast including Philip Seymour Hoffman, William H. Macy, Julianne Moore, Jason Robards, Alfred Molina and Tom Cruise (hugely entertaining and surprisingly off-the-wall as a misogynistic self-help guru – I won't tell you what he believes is king), *Magnolia* is as baffling to some as it is brilliant to others. Yet how can you not be entertained by a film in which the narrator says, "Well, if that was in a movie, I wouldn't believe it"? A scuba diver being dumped on a forest fire by a plane *is* in the movie. Should we believe it?

You may already have heard the story of the diver, since it has had a long life as an urban legend. Here's what is supposed to have happened: a firefighting plane – or sometimes a helicopter, – scoops up water from a lake to drop on a forest fire. However, a scuba diver is swimming in the lake and is accidentally (and without anyone noticing) scooped up with the water before being unceremoniously dumped on the fire. When the blaze is extinguished firefighters are baffled to find the remains of the diver and equipment, miles away from the nearest body of water.

Let's start with the helicopter version. The large, flexible bucket that hangs below the helicopter is called a helibucket and can hold up to 10,000 litres of water – a lot of water. However, the opening on its top (which lets the water in) consists of a 30cm-wide ring with arms radiating out to the bucket material. There is simply no way that a diver with an air tank could get through the opening. The hole at the bottom of the bucket is even smaller, with a diameter of about 15cm. This is to prevent all of the water being dropped at once, which would cause it

to fall uselessly through the burning trees to the forest floor. Instead, the small opening causes the water to fall as a spray cloud, so that it envelops the trees.

Neither could a diver realistically get tangled up on the outside of the bucket, because the helicopter is effectively lifting its maximum load when it carries a full helibucket, so the additional weight of a diver plus equipment would make it unstable. Besides, most divers leave a flag on the surface of the water to alert boaters – and, perhaps, pilots – to their presence.

And as for fire service *airplanes* that scoop up the water, well, that's no more plausible because their intakes are just as small and also have a grille across them.

Divers being dumped on forest fires? That's just plane stupid.

Chilli Sauce Score: $ $ $ $ $

TWISTER

(1996, Dir. Jan de Bont)

The bit where a tornado picks up a petrol tanker

Here's another story that turned out to be (slightly) more of a myth. An audience is watching *Twister* at a Canadian drive-in cinema. Suddenly the screen begins to vibrate and the air is filled with whooshing sounds. People are greatly impressed with the film's SFX until they realise that an actual tornado is approaching. The screen is flattened and the members of the audience flee for their lives… In reality, a tornado did damage a Canadian drive-in which was due to show *Twister*, but not while the film was playing. As you may have guessed, *Twister* is all about tornados and the people who locate and study them, known as storm chasers. The film's effects are pretty special, as a succession of bigger and bigger tornados suck up everything from a cow and a car to a tractor and a speedboat. But what about a fully-laden petrol tanker?

A tornado is a fast-rotating column of air that reaches to the ground from a storm cloud. It is caused when advancing cold air overruns pre-existing warmer humid air. And, like water spinning down a plughole, the rising warmer air twists into a column. Tornados usually have a diameter of between 20 and 100 metres, wind speeds of between 110 and 175 km/h; they generally travel for two to five kilometres, and last for a few minutes. However the biggies are over a kilometre wide, wreak havoc for over 100 kilometres and have winds reaching 480 km/h.

The USA has its tornado alley, a broad swathe of land stretching from Nebraska to Texas and Oklahoma (where the film is set). But the country with the highest number of reported tornados by area is… England. (On a cold and windy 23 November 1981, 105 tornadoes broke out across the country.) Needless to say,

most English tornados are dwarfed by their American cousins. Which leads us to the question of size. The tornado that lifts the petrol tanker in *Twister* is categorized as an F5. This is the highest intensity rating on the Fujita Scale and corresponds to wind speeds up to 512 km/h. The Fujita Scale describes the likely damage from an F5 and it's truly frightening: strong frame houses lifted off foundations and carried considerable distances to disintegrate; automobile-sized missiles fly over 100 metres through the air; trees debarked; steel-reinforced concrete structures badly damaged. In other words, incredible phenomena can and do occur. But is a fully-laden petrol tanker just too incredible?

In theory it's possible. In practice very few tornados are strong enough. There have been many documented cases, including on film, of family cars being lifted several hundred feet into the air. But large vehicles, such as farm machinery, tractors, trains – and petrol tankers – tend to be blown across the ground rather than sucked into the air.

So even though the devastation caused by the tornados in the film is quite true to life, *Twister*'s reality still comes with a twist.

Chilli Sauce Score: ♪♪

"CROCODILE" DUNDEE

(1986, Dir. Peter Faiman)

The bit where Mick Dundee tells the time by the position of the sun

No film requires quotation marks in its title, period. (They were added so that American audiences didn't think that Dundee was actually a crocodile.) Still, no Australian film has grossed more. Paul Hogan plays the eponymous outdoorsman, full of tall tales and native wisdom: who can argue with "Cities are crowded right? If I went and lived in some city, I'd only make it worse"? And Mr Dundee not only tells the time by looking at the sun. He gets it right, down to the minute.

So what do you do if you've left home without a timepiece? First, presuming you're in the northern hemisphere, face south towards the equator. Then, basically, look at the half of the sky across which the sun travels. If the sun is in the exact centre of the sky, it's mid-day. Job done (unless it's daylight savings time when it'll be 1pm). If the sun is not in the centre of the sky, it will be in the eastern half of the sky if it's morning and the western half in the afternoon.

If that's not accurate enough, estimate the number of hours between sunrise and sunset, based on the day before: in Britain, it goes from about eight hours in winter to sixteen at midsummer. Then divide the sun's path into segments from the eastern horizon to the western horizon (or, if you can't see them, where the horizons would be if you could). The number of segments should equal the number of hours in the day. Determine which segment the sun is in and this will tell you how many daylight hours have passed and how many are remaining. If you know the time of sunrise or sunset you can work out the current time.

67

If that's still not accurate enough, count segments by holding the open palm of your hand towards you with your fingers horizontal to the ground. Going hand over hand, follow the line of the sun from the eastern horizon and count how many hands it takes to get to the high point of the sun's path. That number is half a day, so if it took nine hands to get to the high point, and the day is twelve hours long, nine hands would equal six hours. Then you divide the number of hours by the number of hands, in this case six divided by nine. This tells you that each hand represents two-thirds of an hour – forty minutes. So if the sun is four hands from the eastern horizon, multiply that by your hours-per-hand measurement. For example, four times forty minutes equals 160 minutes. So, two hours and forty minutes have passed since sunrise. You can even drill your calculation down to an accuracy of twenty minutes. Instead of using all four fingers to count your segments, tuck two into your palm and just use the other two. There'll be double the number of segments but also double the precision.

So there are a couple of problems with Mr Dundee's method of time-keeping. First, it *is* possible to tell the time pretty accurately by looking at the sun, but only with some nifty fingerwork and number-crunching. And second, he lives in a nice sunny country.

Whereas I live in England.

Chilli Sauce Score: ♪♪♪

THE LAST PICTURE SHOW

(1971, Dir. Peter Bogdanovich)

The bit where Tumbleweed blows through the town of Anarene

In this classic set in the early 1950s, two high school friends (Timothy Bottoms and Jeff Bridges) come of age in a small, isolated town in west Texas. Shot in bleak black and white, *The Last Picture Show* is a compelling study of love and loneliness in a town that is slowly dying. And what better symbol of moral and social drift than tumbleweed blowing down a dusty street? But when was the last time you saw a tangled, rootless bush bounce down your road? Does tumbleweed even exist?

Tumbleweed has become a screen cliché. These days it's usually played for laughs (think of the beginning of another Bridges masterpiece, *The Big Lebowski*). And it is real. The plant, a member of the goosefoot family, grows in dry regions and is also known as Russian thistle, supposedly having been introduced to the southern states of the US by Russian immigrants towards the end of the 19th century. Within 20 years it covered more than a dozen states (at the time it was suggested that a fence be built around the whole state of North Dakota to stop the shrub's advance).

Young tumbleweeds are green and bushy, with small greenish-white or light pink flowers. They grow from one to four feet tall after which they dry out, uproot and get blown along with the wind, which aids the dispersal of their 200,000 seeds. That's why they tumble. Today, tumbleweed storms in the flat and arid southwestern US can involve thousands of bouncing bushes.

Apart from as a movie prop, does this noble shrub have any other uses? Yes – young lads have been known to tie a tumbleweed

to a length of string and fly it like a kite, albeit rather an ugly one. And during the lean years of the Great Depression the youngest and greenest plants were cooked and eaten.

So if you though the tumbleweed was pure fiction, you should eat a slice of humble (tumbleweed) pie.

Chilli Sauce Score: ⟩

WAYNE'S WORLD

(1992, Dir. Penelope Spheeris)

The bit where shooting stars streak across the sky

 It's a serious and profoundly moving film... NOT! *Wayne's World* is Mike Myers' feature film debut, introducing audiences to his special brand of silliness, sight gags and stupidly catchy catchphrases – *Ex-squeeze me? Baking powder? Asphinctersayswhat? We're not worthy! Party on!* Wayne and Garth love to lie on the bonnet of their "Mirthmobile", staring at the night's sky bejewelled with stars – both the stationary and shooting kinds. But are the latter actually stars at all?

No. They're defined as meteors (from the Greek *meteoron* meaning a phenomenon in the sky): basically any matter from space that enters the Earth's atmosphere and becomes luminescent due to atmospheric friction. This happens between 50 and 68 miles above Earth's surface. The term "meteoroid" refers to matter which stays out in space, from grains of space dust to large boulders – in fact, anything smaller than an asteroid or comet. And a meteor*ite* is matter that makes it safely through our atmosphere so as to reach the Earth's surface without having burned up completely. So far, nearly 40,000 meteorites have been found around the world.

However, before you start to muse on how wonderful it is that a noble chunk of rock can find its way through the cold depths of interstellar space into our atmosphere, crashing through its upper reaches in a blaze of glory, all for your private enjoyment... think again. Your meteor is probably space trash. In 1965, there were 555 objects in space made by man's fair hands. Today, there are over 35,000. A good 3,000 of these objects have a use: they're satellites, for example, or the International Space Station. The rest is rubbish – an astronaut's glove, a toolbag, a fridge, etc. And it's all whizzing around the Earth at 32,000 km/h, which can cause serious problems when objects collide. A chip of paint once came off the International Space Station and hit one of the shuttles: it made an eight-centimetre-deep dent in the shuttle's window.

At RAF Fylingdales on the North Yorkshire Moors there's a large radar that keeps track of all objects larger than $10cm^3$. It's one of six such radars around the world – and they're kept busy. There are over 14,000 man-made objects in space larger than a football. And recently 600 new ones were added when two satellites crashed into one another. Each item is given a reference number: no. 33442 is an astronaut's toolbag; no. 00005 is debris from Sputnik 1, the first ever man-made object in space. And the event that the monitoring stations fear most is a cascade, where the debris from one impact sets off a chain-reaction of collisions that could, in theory, knock out Earth's communications.

No way.

Way!

Chilli Sauce Score: ♪ ♪ ♪

MOBY DICK

(1956, Dir. John Huston)

The bit where St. Elmo's fire lights up the Pequod

 No, the crew of Captain Ahab's ship aren't huddled around a glowing TV as they watch the 1985 Brat Pack drama. We'll leave it to Herman Melville, author of the novel *Moby-Dick* to explain.

"Look aloft!" cried Starbuck. "The corpusants! The corpusants!" All the yard-arms were tipped with a pallid fire; and touched at each tri-pointed lightning-rod-end with three tapering white flames, each of the three tall masts was silently burning in that sulphurous air, like three gigantic wax tapers before an altar.

The film of the book faithfully shows this nautical phenomenon. But is it just an old seadog's tale?

St. Elmo's fire is also known as "corpusants", from the Portuguese *corpo santo* meaning "holy body". St. Elmo himself was actually Saint Erasmus of Formiae, who died around 300AD and is venerated as the patron saint of sailors. The phenomenon known as St. Elmo's fire, which can supposedly light up the mast of a ship caught in a thunderstorm, is named after the saint because it is seen by sailors as a sign of heavenly intervention foretelling the end of the storm. And with accounts of it describing blue, heatless and non-consuming flames, sometimes accompanied by a hissing sound, it's no wonder that the fire has been thought throughout history to have otherwordly origins. Yet St. Elmo's fire is very much of this world. Benjamin Franklin first guessed correctly that the "fire" was caused by atmospheric electricity when he wrote in 1749 of a lightning rod that he believed could draw electricity "out of the cloud silently before it could come near enough to strike; and a light would be seen at the point like the sailors' corpuzante."

The phenomenon occurs on sharply pointed objects when the strength of the electrical field in the atmosphere reaches around one thousand volts per centimetre, such as during a thunderstorm. The principle involved is that old physics lesson favourite Ohm's Law, which states that when the electrical potential field is great enough to overcome the resistance of the medium across which it occurs, a current of electrons will result. (Very) basically, these electrons are torn from the air molecules that surround the pointed object in a process called ionization. Then the free electrons, ionized molecules (ions) and air molecules collide, exciting the air molecules into luminosity. The reason this happens around pointed objects is that they deflect lines of electrical force from their normal position and concentrate them around the objects' tips.

St. Elmo's fire has been witnessed on the wingtips of aircraft flying through heavily charged skies, as well as on blades of grass, the horns of cattle and even the weapons of Julius Caesar's army. Caesar wrote in his *Commentaries*, "In the month of February about the second watch of the night, there suddenly arose a thick cloud followed by a shower of hail, and the same night the points of the spears belonging to the Fifth Legion seemed to take fire."

In the film *St Elmo's Fire*, Billy Hicks (Rob Lowe) says, "It's St. Elmo's fire. Electric flashes of light that appear in dark skies out of nowhere. Sailors would guide entire journeys by it, but the joke was on them... there was no fire. There wasn't even a St. Elmo. They made it up. They made it up because they thought they needed it to keep them going when times got tough."

Not so, Billy. The joke is on you.

Chilli Sauce Score: ♪

ICE-COLD IN ALEX

(1958, Dir. J. Lee Thompson)

The bit where Anthony Quayle is dragged down by quicksand

"Worth waiting for." Well it was for Carlsberg, who waited some forty years before using the film's ending, when John Mills downs an ice-cold glass of their beer, in a commercial. The beer was real because the beer substitutes (stunt pints?) just didn't look right. It took fourteen takes and as many glasses of beer to get the shot. Tough life being an actor!

However, the cast of this World War II classic did indeed earn their refreshment, having had to overcome a minefield, a desert and, in the case of Anthony Quayle's German spy, some dreaded quicksand. But does quicksand really exist?

Quicksand is a definite favourite in films, from *Lawrence of Arabia* to *Blazing Saddles,* generating fear, suspense, heroic deeds and agonizing deaths in equal measure. But while some films show quicksand as dry and – well – sandy, others (such as *Ice Cold in Alex*) depict it as wet and muddy. It seems that no one is quite sure what exactly the stuff is. No one that is, apart from Indiana Jones. In *Indiana Jones and the Kingdom of the Crystal Skull*, Indy explains the difference between dry and wet quicksand: "Quicksand is a mix of sand, mud and water, and depending on the viscosity it's not as dangerous as people sometimes think," he says. And you know what? He's not far wrong.

Real quicksand occurs when underground water seeps up and infiltrates an area of sand or silt and, because it rises from below, leaves the top layer of visible sand looking dry. Normal sand can support our weight because friction between the individual grains creates a "force chain" which helps distribute the weight over a wide area. However when water gets in, the grains of sand end

up suspended in the water breaking the force chain. All the same, this generally isn't dangerous because the sand is rarely deep and, even when it is, it's almost impossible to become fully submerged because the human body is far more buoyant in quicksand than it is in water. You just end up bobbing up and down like a cork. That isn't to say quicksand is easy to get out of. If you get stuck and start to kick your legs under the surface, you'll create vacuum pockets that suck at your legs, making it even harder to drag yourself out. So exhaustion, heatstroke and dehydration are actually the biggest threats.

Completely dry quicksand is a different matter entirely – partly because its existence has never been officially confirmed. History is littered with stories of people and animals suddenly disappearing underneath the desert sands. But dry quicksand as a natural phenomenon has never been scientifically observed. It has, however, been replicated in the laboratory, by blowing air through sand, causing the grains to form a very loose structure. When an object is placed on the sand, it collapses in on itself and drags the object under whilst shooting a jet of sand into the air. The theory goes that after a sandstorm it is possible that a mass of sand could settle back on the ground in this type of weakened formation. Along comes an unfortunate traveller, and say goodnight Gracie.

But so far this has only ever been witnessed in the lab. And of course, in the cinema.

Chilli Sauce Score: ♪ ♪

THE EMPEROR WALTZ

(1948, Dir. Billy Wilder)

The bit where echoing Austrian Alps accompany Bing Crosby's singing

In fact this film was shot in Canada, although Billy Wilder had pine trees delivered from California and 4,000 daisies planted, which were then painted blue. Bing Crosby plays an American gramophone salesman who is trying to sell one of his machines to Emperor Franz Joseph I of Austria. In the meantime, he falls in love with Joan Fontaine's Countess Johanna von Stolzenberg-Stolzenberg ("so good they named her twice"). Cue various musical interludes, including one in which the surrounding Alps repeat the end of each line Bing sings. Do echoes really behave like that, bouncing back just the ends of words? And why do some places produce better echoes than others?

Sound waves rebound off objects/walls/mountains. But you don't always get an echo. This is because you need distance. Sound is no slouch, travelling at around 340 metres per second. If you make a noise and the sound waves return in under half a second you won't pick them up as an echo because they're too close to the original sound that you made. (If the sound waves return in a tenth of a second or less, your brain processes this as reverberation of your original sound, making it seem amplified and prolonged – like all that splendid singing you do in the shower).

So, with sound travelling 170 metres every half a second, your object/wall/mountain needs to be at least 85 metres away (counting the distance there and back) for it to produce a distinguishable echo. Even then, you'll only catch the end of whatever you said, as the first part will have returned whilst you're still speaking. Just like Bing – although his mountains were far enough away to produce proper echoes.

Yet distance isn't everything. Scream at the top of your lungs at something even as big as a double-decker bus and you won't get an echo. This is because sound waves leave your mouth in all different directions, so only a small percentage of them would rebound in your direction off a bus. You need objects that are really big, such as large buildings… or mountains. And the more the better: a range of mountains, for example, to bounce back sound waves from all directions. The mountains should ideally not be covered in trees either (take note Mr Wilder). Anything that stops the reflecting surface from being as smooth as possible merely serves to scatter the sound waves.

You also need to keep the mountains free from snow. The amount of reflection depends on the dissimilarity between the medium carrying the sound waves (in this case, air) and the reflecting medium. That's why sound-proofed rooms have soft walls: they're closer in substance to air. Similarly, snow deadens sound. You want hard rock. And not much else: echoes are delicate things. They don't like a lot of surrounding noise, such as might be made by people, traffic or (say) a film orchestra.

So although *The Emperor Waltz* gives a fair reflection of the mechanics of sound reflection, Bing doesn't completely ring true… true… true.

Chilli Sauce Score: 🌶🌶

SHERLOCK HOLMES

(2009, Dir. Guy Ritchie)

The bit where an electric shock sends a man flying through the air

Holmes goes Hollywood, but the result isn't half bad. The sleuth (Robert Downey Jr) and his faithful Watson (Jude Law) are up against the supposedly supernatural Lord Blackwood, his evil schemes and boo-hiss henchmen. 6'11" Canadian professional wrestler Robert Maillet plays one of the latter, and in one fight scene gave Downey Jr a real-life bloody nose. Little Bob gets his own back in the film by prodding big Bob with what looks like a Victorian Taser, sending the giant flying through the air. Could an electric shock really have such an effect on a person?

"Never theorize before you have data. Invariably, you end up twisting facts to suit theories, instead of theories to suit facts," says the great detective. So, we'd better investigate.

If the strange device that Holmes uses is anything like a real Taser then the answer is no. Being "tasered" causes stimulation of the sensory and motor nerves (not surprisingly, given you're hit with up to 50,000 volts), which in turn results in what is termed neuromuscular incapacitation. Taser (the company) lists the common effects of neuromuscular incapacitation as, variously: the subject immediately falling to the ground; the subject screaming; the subject freezing with legs locked; the subject experiencing strong involuntary muscle contractions. They don't mention the subject flying thirty feet backwards through the air – although as Taser actually gets its name from the kids' science-fiction novel *Tom Swift and His Electric Rifle*, you'd have thought this would be an outcome to be desired.

But before we jump to any conclusions, let's follow the

Holmesian technique of looking at all available data. When an electric current passes through a person, the resistance to the flow of electricity that their body presents causes skin and flesh to heat up, resulting in pain and possibly burns. And that's just half the story: electric currents also disrupt the body's nervous system. Under normal circumstances, nerve cells (aka neurons) communicate with each other by creating very low voltage electrical signals in response to chemical compounds called neurotransmitters. When a person is subjected to an electric current, the effect is to override the electrical impulses that are generated by the neurons and to overload the nervous system. That's when neuromuscular incapacitation takes place.

Real problems occur when an electrical current scrambles the signals that keep the heart beating rhythmically, sending it into a condition called fibrillation. A fibrillating heart flutters rather than beats and is ineffective at pumping blood around the body. And this brings us to another instance in films where electricity gives people a huge jolt – the emergency room defibrillator. "Clear!" shouts the medic as the defibrillator pads are applied to the chest of the flat-lining patient, whose body jerks violently before the tale-tell beep-beep of a re-established heartbeat is heard. Yet in real life, patients rarely convulse and jump-start their way back into existence. Besides, defibrillators aren't even used on patients with no heartbeat. Rather they are used to help bring a fibrillating heart into a normal beating pattern.

But there's still more detecting to be done. Because there is one electrical phenomenon that *can* cause a person to be thrown through the air. It's called an arc flash and it's a kind of uncontrolled electrical short circuit where an electric current flows through the air from an exposed live conductor either to another conductor or to ground. A massive amount of energy, in the form of heat, sound and pressure waves, is released during an arc flash. This can indeed blow someone through the air, although they are also likely to be set on fire by the heat that is

released, which can reach four times the temperature of the sun.

So, even if the device which Holmes uses to prod the giant goon could produce an arc flash, the venerable detective would surely have been subject to the same blast of energy as his adversary.

Which would leave little more than Sherlock's bones.

Chilli Sauce Score:))))

300

(2007, Dir. Zack Snyder)

The bit where the moon appears much larger than usual

It's unusual for a film to end with all of its heroes being slain. But even today's Hollywood hasn't the brass neck to alter the result of one of Ancient Greece's most famous battles. Gerard Butler buffs up to play King Leonidas of Sparta, leading 300 warriors to face the small matter of 100,000 Persians in the Battle of Thermopylae. Before embarking on his daring mission, Leonidas goes to consult a group of priests called the Ephors. As the King climbs up to their temple, a massive moon rises behind a rocky bluff. But can the moon really appear larger than normal in the sky?

The moon does indeed move closer and farther away to the Earth during its elliptical orbit, but not by enough to alter its perceived size in the sky. At its closest, the centre of the moon is 363,293 kilometres away. At its farthest, the distance is 405,506 kilometres. (The moon is actually moving away from us at the rate of some four and a half centimetres a year.)

But across the world and throughout history people have perceived the moon as sometimes being larger than normal. It's not, as some believe, because of atmospheric conditions and light diffusion, because the phenomenon occurs in many different kinds of conditions. But there is a common factor. The moon is always close to the horizon. Take Friday 24 June 2005, when the moon appeared larger than at any time for the previous twenty years. It also appeared at its lowest in the sky over the same period. The moon's closeness to the horizon is important because its increased size is actually an optical illusion: use a ruler to measure the moon's apparent width on any night at any point of the sky and you'll see that it's always the same.

One theory offered to explain this illusion is that we judge the size of an object by comparing it to things surrounding it. When the moon is high in the sky, we subconsciously compare it to the vast blackness around it, and so it appears smaller. However, when the moon is close to the horizon we compare it to whatever's on the horizon with it, such as houses, trees or a ship. Because distance makes these things appear small, the moon appears much larger in comparison.

This theory seems to stand up when you look at a low moon through a tube made from a rolled-up piece of paper. Without anything else in view, the moon looks the same size as it would higher up in the sky. But airline pilots also perceive a larger moon when it's near the horizon, even though they have no visual cues on the ground.

However, there is an alternative theory that was first proposed by the Egyptian astronomer Ptolemy in the second century AD. Ptolemy suggested that we perceive the sky as a slightly flattened dome rather than the true hemisphere that it is. Therefore, our brains believe that objects on the horizon are father away than those overhead in the flattened area of the sky. And, when we see an object of a certain size when it's far away, we believe that it's bigger than something of the same size that is closer to us. So, as in *300*, the moon can appear larger. But whereas the film's makers created a much bigger moon, in real life the effect is an illusion.

Which must be the only time that nature has faked what Hollywood did for real.

Chilli Sauce Score: ♪♪

THE LOVELY BONES

(2009, Dir. Peter Jackson)

The bit where a falling icicle kills a man

Peter Jackson takes time out from rings and hobbits to direct this… well it's pretty hard to categorize what hovers between sentimental drama, creepy horror and ethereal mystery. Critics and audiences couldn't decide what to make of it either, however wonderful it looks. A fourteen-year-old girl is murdered by her neighbour and watches her family from Heaven, while attempting to get someone to find her lost body. Near the end, murderous neighbour George Harvey gets his comeuppance when an icicle falls from a tree and hits him, causing him to fall into a ravine. But really, what are the chances?

An icicle is formed when water from melting snow drips down from an object and some of the water freezes before it falls to the ground. As more water continues to flow down the icicle, so the icicle grows. That's the simple version. However, all icicles have a universal geometric shape and this is actually caused by heat. As a thin layer of water runs down the icicle, heat is diffused away from the ice, causing an updraft of air. The rising air removes heat from the layer of water, some of which freezes and causes the icicle to get thicker and to elongate.

And icicles can get very long indeed. In 2010, during Britain's coldest winter in 30 years, an icicle formed below the Dulnain Bridge over the River Spey in Grantown, Invernessshire, that measured 27 feet long. Was it the world's longest? Nobody knows, as only a small proportion of icicles have their length recorded. And this could well be because standing underneath them really is a deadly pursuit.

If you think that the coldest winter in Britain for 30 years was a touch chilly, imagine what it must have been like in Russia. It was

the same year, 2010, but in Russia that meant icicles hanging from virtually every building. Sometimes they'd fall, and occasionally they'd fall onto unsuspecting pedestrians. Reports suggest that dozens of people across Russia were killed by icicles. In St Petersburg alone there were five fatalities, and 150 people were injured, including a baby when an icicle plunged into its pram. And in Moscow the danger was such that mountaineers were hired to climb buildings and safely knock icicles to the ground.

Of course, injurious icicles aren't confined to Russia. In 1903, the *New York Times* carried a story of a man from Michigan called Charles Daniels "who was killed last night by a huge icicle which fell upon him as he was making rounds and cut off the top of his head". Further back, in 1776, a son of a Parish clerk in Devonshire was also killed by a falling icicle. His epitaph reads, "Bless my eyes, Here he lies, In a Sad Pickle, Kill'd by an Icicle". And in present day USA, the threat of icicles falling hundreds of feet from skyscrapers, coupled with lawyers who would encourage you to sue if so much as an ice cube fell on your head, has led to the invention of heated gutters to prevent icicles from forming in the first place.

Proving that icicles killing people is indeed the cold hard truth.

Chilli Sauce Score: 🌶

TRANSPORT

"We might have to wait a minute for the church to get out the way."

Deliverance

EASY RIDER

(1969, Dir. Dennis Hopper)

The bit where Fonda and Hopper ride bikes with very small fuel tanks

 As well as featuring a couple of very cool choppers, *Easy Rider* kick-started the career of one Jack Nicholson as well as the whole American New Wave cinema of the 1970s. Fonda and Hopper are Captain America and Billy, riding across the southern United States in search of freedom. As Fonda admits towards the end of the film, "We blew it." That's hardly surprising when the petrol tanks on their bikes look like they couldn't take them to the end of the drive before running out of fuel.

Chopper motorcycles first made an appearance in the 1950s, when owners of American bikes tried to match the speed of the more powerful UK machines by "chopping" off everything that compromised performance. So out went seat springs, windscreens, indicators, horns and even front brakes. But it wasn't all about taking things away. The chopper's distinctive elongated front forks were added because they improved the ride of the bike after its suspension had been reduced. Similarly, the chopper's improved acceleration meant that passengers could easily fall off the back. Hence the heightened seat backs.

In the 1960s and 70s, chopper customization evolved from a need for speed to a need for some serious showing off. Bikes became less "eat my dust" and more "look at me". And the choppers in *Easy Rider* epitomize the sacrifice of function for form: arguably a mistake, seeing as they were meant to carry their riders from Los Angeles all the way to New Orleans.

Peter Fonda had purchased some early 1950s Harley-Davidsons at a police auction and it was from these that the famous bikes used in the film were born. Beautiful and cool as

89

hell: yes. Practical for a long journey: no. Take Captain America's machine. Chrome looks great, but a chromed frame would get beaten up pretty quick. And those drop handlebars would have had the blood draining from Fonda's fingers quicker than the fuel from both bikes' ridiculously small petrol tanks.

And these tanks are the main problem. They look great but the 'peanut' tanks would have held no more than two and a half gallons each. (And that's before Captain America shoved a tube full of drug money into his tank.) So with a reduced fuel capacity, an estimated 35-40 miles per gallon (making around 75 miles per tank) and some 1892 miles of road between Los Angeles and New Orleans, we're talking at least 25 fuel stops – assuming that in 1969 there actually were gas stations no more than 75 miles apart along the entirety of America's southern highways network.

Otherwise, it wouldn't be just Captain America and Billy who were running on fumes.

Chilli Sauce Score: ♪ ♪ ♪ ♪

UNSTOPPABLE

(2010, Dir. Tony Scott)

The bit where Denzel Washington tries to stop a runaway train

The plot is about as linear as the mode of transport it concerns. Driverless freight train runs away down the tracks. Veteran engineer (Washington) and newbie colleague (Chris Pine) try to stop it. But it's a testament to Tony Scott's thunderous direction and sparing use of CGI that the film more than chugs along. Matters are helped by the fact that the train is pulling freight cars full of dangerous chemicals towards a sharply-curved viaduct above fuel storage tanks in the middle of a city. We all know that the rogue locomotive isn't going to live up to the film's title. Even so, it's still a tremendously entertaining ride.

So what exactly is the best way of stopping tons of train? Well, what historical precedents there are suggest it's probably best not to let one of the things go in the first place. As recently as 2010, an unmanned engineering train became detached from its towing train on the London Underground's Northern Line and ran for four miles and through six stops before it came to a halt – and then only because it reached a slight incline. Other trains had to be cleared out of its way while the train directly in front of the runaway ran at full speed, without stopping and with all its passengers told to move towards the front.

Just over fifty years earlier in 1959, a runaway fifteen-car train ended up hitting a Union Pacific depot in Olympia in the US state of Washington, killing one person and injuring twenty others.Such was the force of the impact that the train went straight through the building to destroy half a city block on the other side and cause damage costing $250,000. An investigation

into the accident found that the train's crew had uncoupled fifteen cars (weighing 900 tons) from the locomotive without properly setting handbrakes or airbrakes on the cars, and then left them unattended. The cars being situated on a slight downhill gradient, they started coasting down the slope towards Olympia and reached speeds of between 48 and 96 km/h before hitting the depot. The investigation also criticized the absence of derail switches on the line, which (as you might guess) are designed to derail the wheels of a train as it passes over the switch.

In *Unstoppable*, the rogue locomotive is so heavy and moves so fast that it smashes through a derail switch as if the switch had been rustled up by the bods on *Blue Peter* using an empty cereal packet and some double-sided sticky tape. But that, of course, is not the only attempt that's made to stop the train. Two engines hooked up together are driven in front of the runaway to try and slow it down, whilst a railroad employee is lowered by helicopter onto the speeding train's cab. Needless to say the plan doesn't work. Then Washington and Pine run another locomotive backwards along the line in an attempt to catch the runaway from behind and slow it down. An "attempt" is all it is. The police then abort a plan to shoot a fuel cutoff switch on the side of the train from the side of the track. But fear not, our daring duo do manage to stop the train eventually. You'll just have to watch the film to find out how.

But it's not the same way they brought the real runaway train that inspired the film to a halt. Because *Unstoppable* is indeed "inspired by true events". In 2001, an unmanned forty-seven car freight train CSX Engine 8888 went on a journey of sixty-six miles through Ohio. As in the film, the incident began with the train's driver doing the just-a-little-bit-foolhardy thing of jumping out of the locomotive while it was slowly moving, to reset a trackside switch, with predictable results. As in the film, some of the freight cars contained the hazardous chemical phenol. And as in the film, a derail switch failed to stop the runaway.

Unlike in *Unstoppable*, the police did actually shoot at the fuel cutoff button, although this didn't work because the button had to be pressed for several seconds to work. And unlike in the film, a pursuing train was able to couple onto the locomotive to slow it down enough so that a train driver could run alongside the tracks, jump aboard the cab and stop the engine.

So runaway trains can be brought to a halt, albeit with some difficulty. Meanwhile the best thing to do is just to… run away.

Chilli Sauce Score: ♪♪

GENEVIEVE

(1953, Dir. Henry Cornelius)

The bit where Kenneth More gets his car's wheels stuck in tramlines

One of Britain's best loved post-war comedies about the London to Brighton veteran car rally was actually directed by a South African, scored by an American harmonica player (Larry Adler), and starred two foreign-built 1904 cars, a Dutch Spyker and a French Darracq, the eponymous Genevieve, which to this day still completes the annual London to Brighton rally. Yet the film itself is British down to its tyre valves, a gentle comedy with an even gentler romance offset by a mad dash to be the first car across Westminster Bridge.

It's a race that Kenneth More and the lovely, late lamented Kay Kendall look set to win until their Spyker gets its tyres wedged into tramlines, diverting the car away from the bridge and leaving John Gregson, Dinah Sheridan and of course Genevieve to claim first place. The tyre-and-tramline combo is a classic comedy stunt. But are they also a comedy con, or did cars and their hapless drivers really find themselves being tramlined in all directions?

It seems that the film takes a couple of diversions from the truth. Tramlines are composed of a recessed rail, rather than simply a groove in the road, and the gaps either side of the rail are simply too narrow for a car's wheels (even those as thin as a vintage car's) to become wedged. And if your tyre did get caught, you wouldn't have had to be Stirling Moss to steer it out again.

However, that isn't to say that tramlines didn't and don't present a hazard for road users. There is one mode of transport whose tyres are just about the right size to get stuck in the tracks: the humble bicycle. Over the years many cyclists have found that, as they bowled along the high street with their front-mounted

basket full of shopping, the front tyre has disappeared into the chasm of doom never to return. The result? A buckled wheel, a dozen broken eggs and two bruised buttocks.

Now that really is classic comedy.

Chilli Sauce Score: ♪♪♪♪

THUNDERBALL

(1965, Dir. Terence Young)

The bit where Bond travels by jetpack

The name "Thunderball" comes from the term used by US soldiers for the mushroom cloud produced by an atomic bomb. And there certainly is an explosion of vehicular activity in this fourth Bond offering, including 007's Aston Martin DB5; a 1965 convertible Ford Mustang; a 1957 Ford Fairlane 500 Skyliner; a 1965 Lincoln Continental convertible; a Triumph Herald Cabriolet; a BSA 650cc A65L Lightning motorbike; the *Disco Volante* hydrofoil yacht; a Sikorsky S-62 helicopter; a Boeing B-17 plane; and an Avro Vulcan B.1 bomber; not to mention speedboats and underwater tow sleds. And let's not forget the film's pre-title sequence in which Bond kills a SPECTRE agent dressed as a widow, before escaping by strapping on a jetpack and flying off. But surely if jetpacks were a reality in the 1960s, by now we'd all be using them to pop down to Tesco.

The name of Scottish indie rock band "We Were Promised Jetpacks" seems to say it all. That highly anticipated future means of transportation, as depicted in a thousand comic books, used by Buck Rogers and (it was surely only a matter of time) everyone else… is nowhere to be seen. So was the intro to *Thunderball* mere camera trickery and, if not, why hasn't the jetpack ever lifted off as a viable vehicle?

Actually the film's jetpack flight was for real… as jetpacks themselves are for real. During the 1950s, the American military looked seriously at developing a Small Rocket Lift Device to enable soldiers to overcome difficult terrain and waterways. Bell Aerosystems was the company commissioned with designing and building the device, and the result was the Bell Aerosystems Rocket Belt: the very model that was used in *Thunderball*. The

jetpack consisted of a glass-plastic frame attached to which were two cylinders of hydrogen peroxide and one of nitrogen. Within the engine, the nitrogen pressed the hydrogen peroxide onto a catalyst which decomposed the hydrogen peroxide. This resulted in a mixture of steam and oxygen with a temperature of about 740°C that blasted out of two nozzles, providing thrust. The pilot/aeronaut/jetpacker/nutjob controlled the device by means of a lever in each hand: left lever for direction, right lever for thrust. Test flights were conducted in a large hangar with the jet pack tethered to the ground to stop it whizzing around like a deflating balloon.

On 20 April 1961 the first free flight of a jetpack took place near Niagara Falls, when Harold Graham reached the dizzying height of 1.2 metres before flying forward at the eye-watering speed of 10 km/h for the unbelievable distance of just under 35 metres. The entire flight lasted 13 seconds. Still it was a start. And things improved to the extent that a height of 10 metres, a distance of 120 metres and a top speed of 55 km/h were all achieved. However one major problem remained, one which saw the American military withdraw its funding for the project. The maximum duration of flight for the Rocket Belt (owing to the amount of fuel it could carry) was a measly 21 seconds, with a timer set to buzz in the pilot's helmet after 15 seconds to remind him to land. The Rocket Belt's supersonic exhaust jet also made a high-pitched 130-decibel screech (nothing like the manly roar in the film), which meant that people definitely knew you were coming – not great if they had machineguns. So the jetpack remained a kind of novelty, symbolised by its use in *Thunderball* and in the opening ceremony of the Los Angeles Olympic games in 1984.

However for some, talk of a jetpack that can be used for recreation is more than hot air. New Zealand inventor Glenn Martin has spent 30 years developing a new jetpack for the 21st century. Utilising a state-of-the-art carbon-fibre frame and Kevlar

rotors, the Martin Jetpack holds enough fuel for 30 minutes and can theoretically reach speeds of up to 100 km/h. During field tests in May 2011, a manned jetpack reached a height of 5,000 ft. And if further tests are successful you should be able to pick one up for around $100,000. However, before you start saving up and looking forward to an extra half an hour in bed before strapping on your jetpack and rising above the rat race on your way to work, you should know that the Martin Jetpack is restricted to non-urban airspace.

Yes, we were promised jetpacks. But it looks like we might have to wait a while longer.

Chilli Sauce Score: ♪♪

THE GENERAL

(1927, Dir. Clyde Bruckman and Buster
Keaton)

The bit where Buster Keaton sits on the wheel of a moving steam train

The Great Stone Face has never ceased to amaze audiences with his ability to maintain the most deadpan of expressions whilst being exposed to extreme physical danger. *The General* is recognised as one of cinema's finest films. And it certainly contains many of Keaton's most perilous action sequences. But was his most iconic stunt faked?

This silent film is based on a real incident during the American Civil War. In 1862 volunteers from the Union Army stole a train, sabotaging the line, burning bridges and cutting telegraph lines as they went. Meanwhile Confederate soldiers pursued them using other locomotives, one of which was driven in reverse. This story of derring-do formed the basis for *The General* and for many of Keaton's locomotive-based stunts.

These include clambering all over the outside of a moving train, sitting just above the rails on the engine's "cowcatcher" and dodging cannon fire. No CGI, no problem. One of the more innocuous stunts involved Keaton sitting on one of the connecting rods that drive the train's wheels as it slowly pulled away. No hair-raising speed or bone-crunching crash, just Stone Face looking stone-faced as he goes gently up and down and the train rolls into the engine shed. The sequence doesn't even look like a stunt, yet there was one thing that made it the most dangerous one of all. It's called "wheel slip" and it occasionally occurs when a train's wheels lose traction on the rails and spin furiously. If it had happened when the locomotive moved off with Keaton sitting on one of the connecting rods, Buster's body would have been busted into little pieces.

When the first steel train tracks and steel wheels were introduced, certain smart alecs scoffed that wheel slip would happen all the time: the engines were too heavy and the rails too slippery for traction to take place. Yet the opposite turned out to be the case, as the steel molecules when pressed together created a cohesive force that greatly assisted traction. And the heavier the locomotive (the Union Pacific's 'Big Boys' delivered a weight of 250,000 kilos onto their drive wheels), the greater the adhesion.

Yet we've all heard of leaves on the line and the havoc they can cause. Rails that are wet and greasy decrease traction no matter how heavy the locomotive. This can happen when a train moves off or when it's travelling at speed, and locomotives used to have a sandbox at the front which deposited sand onto the rails to help increase grip until the cohesive force of steel on steel was restored. Sand is still used today alongside computerized traction control systems.

So the presence of anti-slip measures goes to show that wheel slip can and does occur. Look carefully and you'll see that it even happens for real in a couple of scenes in *The General*. And this makes Keaton's most memorable of stunts also one of his maddest. He did it for real and what he did took a lot of guts.

It's just lucky we didn't end up seeing them.

Chilli Sauce Score: ♪

DELIVERANCE

(1972, Dir. John Boorman)

The bit where a truck carries a church

 If you ever thought that Burt Reynolds' acting ability was confined to driving a black Trans Am from road movie sequel to road movie sequel (downhill all the way), then you may be surprised by his turn as Lewis, one of four Atlanta businessmen on a canoe trip down through the Georgia wilderness. Burt can actually act. Full of memorably disturbing moments, from banjo-plucking inbreds to death by crossbow, *Deliverance* shows that not all buddy bonding films are bereft of balls. But when a complete church is moved on the back of a truck, isn't the director also transporting us away from the truth?

This feat of transportation happens near the end of the film, when the depleted group finally reaches its destination: the town of Aintry, which is being evacuated before the river valley in which it lies is flooded. A truck with a complete church on its flatbed makes its way down the road. The symbolic desertion of God from both the town and the men is clear. Less so is how a whole building can be moved without its falling to pieces.

But it can be done.

Aside from the immediate threat of flooding, there are other reasons why a building's owners might want to relocate it. For many it's the prospect of a ten-lane motorway ploughing through the front room, although for some it's just about moving somewhere nicer (imagine being able to pluck up your inner-city dwelling and plonk it down in the middle of the countryside). If done shrewdly, the increase in value of a relocated property can easily outstrip the cost of moving. And it isn't just houses that have upped sticks (or bricks) and moved across the world. In 1999, a 2,500-ton lighthouse built in 1870 was moved inland in North Carolina to protect it from land erosion. In 2004, the 15,000-ton Fu Gang Building in China was moved 35 metres and became the heaviest building ever moved. And in 2006, an 11-metres tall statue of Ramses II was relocated in Cairo, proving that not even 3,200 year-old pharaohs are safe from the "shack draggers", as structural movers are known.

The moving process begins with an analysis of the building's design and a calculation of its weight. Then excavation takes place beneath the structure, and support jacks are installed before steel beams are inserted which bear the entire load. Hydraulic jacks raise the structure off its original foundations and rubber-tyred "dollies" are placed under the building and attached to the steel beams. And off it goes. Slowly. Once the building arrives at its destination, it's a simple case of lowering the structure onto its freshly prepared foundations. Of course, accidents do happen. Overhead power lines, snowstorms, failed brakes, low bridges and buildings falling off their trucks can all make life difficult for the shack draggers.

But at least if you're moving a church, you've somewhere to go to pray for help.

Chilli Sauce Score: 🌶

LAWRENCE OF ARABIA

(1962, Dir. David Lean)

The bit where train runs on tracks across the desert

Well it does for a bit, until Lawrence and the Arabs blow it to pieces. Noël Coward once said that if Peter O'Toole looked any lovelier in the film they'd have had to call it Florence of Arabia. Then again, David Lean could make a camel seem attractive. Never has sand looked more alluring or more deadly. The sheer sun-pummelled and wind-blown scale of the Nefud and Sinai deserts is truly awe-inspiring... and makes you wonder how exactly train tracks can run across the sand without being swallowed up.

The tracks in the film and in real life belong to the Hejaz (or Hijaz) railway, which links Damascus with the holy cities of Medina and Mecca. Before the railway opened in 1908, those making the hajj (pilgrimage) from Damascus to Mecca could expect their journey to take 40 to 50 days across some very inhospitable terrain. The new railway was announced by Abdul Hamid, Caliph of Islam and Sultan of the Ottoman Empire, and the route planned by Turkish engineer Haji Mukhtar Bey (he simply followed a caravan, safe in the knowledge that caravans would have found the easiest course over centuries of pilgrimage).

The line was actually built by a German engineer, Messner, who commanded a team comprising 17 Turks, 12 Germans, 5 Italians, 5 Frenchmen, 2 Austrians, 1 Belgian and 1 Greek... and 5,630 soldiers from the Turkish Army. And the railway was German engineering at its best: the rails were secured to steel ties weighing 40 kg each and lying on a 30 centimetre-deep crushed rock ballast which rested on a gravel embankment. This kept the line from sinking into the desert – but of more concern was the shifting, wind-blown sand. In one recent test, a 50 km/h wind was shown to move 2,700

kg of sand over a railway line. But that's a mere breeze compared to the thunderous gales that rip through the desert, piling dunes up to 300 metres high. One European traveller described conditions thus: "Brown walls of cloud rushed changelessly upon us with a loud grinding sound. It struck, wrapping about us a blanket of dust and stinging grains of sand, twisting and turning in violent eddies. Camels were sometimes blown completely around. Small trees were torn up and flung at us."

When the line was built, the solution to the threat of sandstorms was to cover some areas of the surrounding sand with clay and to build barriers made from rocks. And for the most part it worked. When plans were made in the 1960s to resurrect the railway, engineers found that great stretches of uncovered and unrusted line still ran true across the desert – although time had allowed sand to accumulate over some parts of the track in dunes up to 5 metres high and 300 metres long.

The perils of the Nefud and Sinai deserts notwithstanding, the greatest threat to the Hejaz railway was T.E. Lawrence and the Arab tribesmen. During World War I, the railway's existence enabled the Turks to deliver their military forces into the heart of the Arabian Peninsula. Lawrence was quick to identify the railway's value to the Turkish army. "Our ideal," he wrote, "was to keep [the Turk's] railroad just working, but only just, with the maximum loss and discomfort."

The attacks on the railway began and the winds of change, rather than those of sand, began to blow through Arab history.

Chilli Sauce Score:

DUEL

(1971, Dir. Steven Spielberg)

The bit where a fuel tanker outruns a car at 95mph

Dennis Weaver plays David Mann, an electronics salesman who is pursued across the California desert by the meanest of machines: an ugly fuel tanker with a faceless, psychotic driver at the wheel. Steven Spielberg's first feature film (albeit made for TV) is basically *Jaws* on wheels: man (or in this case, Mann) vs monster – a connection between the two films that the director made explicit by taking the primordial groan that accompanies the tanker as it crashes over a cliff and reusing it in *Jaws,* when the shark's carcass sinks to the bottom of the ocean. However, just as Spielberg pushed the boundaries of believability with his great white, so he does with his grimy tanker. At one point Weaver's car shows 95mph (153 km/h) on its speedometer as the tanker closes in from behind. But isn't that a bit *fast* for a truck?

The tanker in question is a Peterbilt. Spielberg chose that particular make because its round headlights and split windscreen looked like a face, adding to the vehicle's anthropomorphic malice. The main model used in the film, and the one destroyed at the end, was a 1955 (or 1956 depending on who you talk to) Peterbilt 281. When further scenes were needed to stretch out the TV film for its release in cinemas, a 1964 Peterbilt 351 was used. However the only truck that survives from the filming is a 1960 Peterbilt 281, a spare which is never actually seen in the film. The surviving 281's original engine was called a Cummins 262, which had six straight cylinders, a turbo and performance of 262 bhp (boiler horsepower). Its current engine is a Cummins NTC 350 with performance of 350 bhp. A recent owner of the 281 managed to get it up to a speed of 74 mph (118 km/h). So from this we can

assume that the lesser-powered original engine could not have taken the tanker (whether laden or unladen with fuel) anywhere near 95 mph.

But that's not to say that other trucks don't reach such speeds. Some do for sport. Truck racing competitions have been held in the UK for twenty-five years, the attraction for drivers and spectators alike being that, when big rigs rip round tracks designed for small cars, the races are extremely close in all respects. Trailers aren't attached to the trucks (now that *would* be something) and the vehicles have their engines, brakes and just about everything else modified. Yet, as one novice driver noted, you can do anything you want to a truck but it's still "like driving a block of flats from the sixth floor". And the trucks are quick – although regulations state that, as each one weighs in excess of 5,500kg, they're not allowed to race faster than 100mph. But boy can they accelerate, with their 12-litre turbocharged engines producing over 1000 horsepower and getting them to 100mph faster than a Porsche 911. However for top speed, all other trucks eat the dust of an American monster called Shockwave. Powered by three jet engines, Shockwave generates 36,000 horsepower and has been clocked at 376mph.

It makes the petrol tanker in *Duel* seem more like a milk float.

Chilli Sauce Score: ♪ ♪ ♪ ♪

THE SEVEN YEAR ITCH

(1955, Dir. Billy Wilder)

The bit where Marilyn Monroe's dress gets blown about in an updraught from the subway

 "Isn't it delicious?" coos Monroe as the white dress (which was recently auctioned for £2.8m) billows up around her legs. And delicious she certainly is, although the iconic full-length image of Monroe on the New York subway grate was only ever used as a publicity photograph: in the film we just see shots of her legs and then her reaction. The film (in which Tom Ewell's character, a professional book reader, sends his family away from the city and the summer heat but ends up fantasizing about the young woman who's moved in upstairs) is based on a play; but is there more truth in the subway grate scene?

The scene was originally filmed during the early hours of the morning at the corner of Lexington Avenue and 52nd Street in New York. However, because the filming location had been publicised beforehand, a crowd of over one thousand people turned up to get a glimpse of one of the world's most famous stars. Their wolf-whistling and cheering not only rendered each take unusable but was also partly to blame for the break-down (after considerably less than seven years) of the marriage between Monroe and baseball legend Joe DiMaggio. As a result the sidewalk location was recreated and the scene was re-shot in the studio. That's the one we see in the film. But do the grates over the real New York subway produce such potentially revealing gusts of air?

Well, they certainly produce a big enough breeze to lift bears, giraffes and even a 25-foot-high Loch Ness monster into the air.

Hang on a minute. What?

I'm talking about inflatable art. Street artist Joshua Allen

Harris takes bin liners and carrier bags, cuts them into the shapes of giant animals and then tapes them to subway grates on New York's sidewalks. When a train passes underneath, gusts of air inflate what look like discarded plastic bags and transform them into swaying, dancing, writhing beasts before the breeze dies down and the animals die too.

However the grates aren't always great. They are flush with the ground and the shafts they cover open directly onto the stations below. So when it rains heavily, as it did on 8 August 2007 when three inches of rain fell in under an hour, the subway system can become flooded. The answer to this has been a $31 million flood-prevention plan, including redesigned grates that have been lifted off the sidewalk and incorporated into pieces of street furniture and even sculptures with beautiful lines and sweeping curves.

A bit like Ms Monroe herself.

Chilli Sauce Score:)

PARIS, TEXAS

(1984, Dir. Wim Wenders)

The bit where a freight train takes a very long time to pass

 This poetic tale of a lost man, his brother and the wife and child he deserted lingers in the memory long after its rueful images of the sprawling Texan landscape have vanished. Its unassuming yet undeniable emotional power moved not one but two Scottish rock bands, Texas and Travis, to use it as the inspiration for their names. It is said that no film can be all bad that has veteran character actor Harry Dean Stanton in it. And this film is almost all good. But surely that freight train is far too long?

Travis (Harry Dean Stanton) and his brother Walt (Dean Stockwell) are sitting in Walt's car at a train-crossing. As they talk about Travis' son Hunter, a freight train rattles past. It takes around one minute and fifteen seconds for the scene to play out, and assuming the train is travelling at around 50 km/h, that puts its length at just about 1000 metres. Which seems very long.

However this turns out to nothing compared to the length of the longest freight train ever recorded. This train was assembled in 2001 by the company BHP Iron Ore for a one-off journey from its Newman mine to Port Hedland in Western Australia – a distance of 274 km. It consisted of 682 wagons holding 82,262 tonnes of iron ore and was pulled and pushed by 8 massive diesel-electric locomotives. Its length totalled some 7.25 km. BHP Iron Ore created the train in order to test a set-up in which locomotives are evenly situated along the train's length. In this case the set-up was 2 locomotives, 166 wagons, 2 locomotives, 168 wagons, 2 locomotives, 168 wagons, 1 locomotive, 180 wagons, 1 locomotive. And just one driver. The train was filmed on its journey, and I can confirm that it takes 7 minutes and 55 seconds to go by the camera. The train is very impressive. The footage of it going past is very boring.

So yes, trains can be as long as the one in *Paris, Texas* – indeed, far longer. But luckily Wim Wenders decided to include some other things in his film too.

Chilli Sauce Score: ♪

AIRPLANE!

(1980, Dir. Jim Abrahams, David Zucker
and Jerry Zucker)

The bit where an inflatable autopilot flies the plane

 Unlike *"Crocodile" Dundee*, here the punctuation seems entirely appropriate. *Airplane!* is one of the most wildly funny films ever made, thanks in no small part to the dead-pan brilliance of Leslie Nielsen. TransAmerican flight 209 to Chicago gets caught in a blizzard of corny jokes, sight gags and disaster movie clichés. The crew comes down with food poisoning and, before a traumatized ex-fighter pilot takes the controls, the autopilot helps to fly the plane. Only this autopilot is inflatable, dressed in uniform and called Otto.

Surely real autopilots are a bit more sophisticated? Of course they are… and stop calling me Shirley. The proper name for an autopilot is an automatic flight control system (AFCS), although 'Otto' sounds a lot better. And they aren't a particularly modern invention. In fact it was in 1914 that an American, Lawrence Sperry, first installed such a device in an aircraft to help stabilise it. Sperry's device consisted of four gyroscopes, and his method of testing it was for him and his co-pilot to climb out onto the wings of the airplane in midair. The gyroscopes did their job and kept the plane level. Thus was born the autopilot, and first among many subsequent flying firsts, from the first night flight to the first round-the-world flight.

Autopilots work by using the three types of control surfaces on an aircraft that determine its stability. These are, first, the elevators on the tail of the plane that control its pitch by push-ing its nose and tail up or down. Then there's the rudder, also on the tail. This controls the yaw, which is when the aircraft turns left or right. Finally the ailerons (flaps) on the back edge of each wing control how the airplane rolls by tilting the wings. A modern autopilot uses a computer linked to sensors on all of the airplane's control surfaces, while also collecting data from other instruments including an altimeter, compass, airspeed indicator and Global Positioning System. The computer assimilates all this data and compares it to a set of control modes and settings. Then if required, the computer sends signals to servos controlling the motors and hydraulics that move the control surfaces, helping the aircraft maintain a correct course, altitude and attitude. This produces a new set of data which is sent back to the computer, and the whole process starts again. Today's autopilots are so effective that they are used routinely in flights, not only in emergencies. They do occasionally fail but, because every autopilot incorporates a failsafe, if one does go wrong the pilot can always override it and return his or her aircraft to manual control.

Problems that affect autopilots include faulty sensors or a servo failure. However, no incident has yet been reported of an autopilot suffering a puncture.

Chilli Sauce Score:)))))

LORDS OF DOGTOWN

(2005, Dir. Catherine Hardwicke)

The bit where skateboards catch air in a swimming pool

 Heath Ledger will always be remembered for playing the Joker in *The Dark Knight* and Ennis Del Mar in *Brokeback Mountain*. Could two roles be any more different? But pretty much every performance he gave is worth remembering, including this one as surf and skateboard shop owner, Skip Engblom, who also manages a team of young skaters, the Z-Boys. The film tells the true story of the infamous team and how they revolutionized skateboarding in 1970s California. But did these dudes really learn their tricks by skating in empty swimming pools?

Nobody can remember who invented the first skateboard, but the idea originated in the 1950s amongst California surfers who thought it might be fun to try and surf on land. The first skateboards were wooden boxes with clay rollerskate wheels attached to the bottom. Boxes soon turned to boards but, as long the clay wheels remained, the skateboards were far from safe and were mostly used as a mode of transport rather than for tricks. Nobody thought to skate anything but pavements and the only stunts anyone tried were simple balancing acts.

However in 1972, more durable and safer urethane wheels were introduced and skateboarding's popularity was resurrected amongst surfers – including a gang of youngsters from a run-down area between Venice Beach and Santa Monica known as Dogtown. In the same year, Skip Engblom, Jeff Ho and Craig Stecyk started up a surf shop called Jeff Ho and Zephyr Surfboard Productions in the middle of Dogtown. The shop soon became a focal point for the Dogtown surfer/skaters, and went on to sponsor the Zephyr Competition Skate Team.

The Z-Boys, as they were known, skated like no one else.

Led by Tony Alva and Jay Adams, they evolved their new way of skating on the sloping asphalt playgrounds of some of the local hill-bound schools. The asphalt banks acted like waves, enabling the skaters to use surfing techniques, riding low with an arm outstretched for balance and even dragging their hand along the ground like surfer Larry Bertlemann, who was the first to drag his fingers along a wave as he surfed, and after whom the skateboarding move 'the Burt' is named.

But the Z-Boys found another place to practice, one which literally made skateboarding take off: swimming pools. In the mid-1970s, California suffered one of the most severe droughts in its history. To conserve water, many private pools around Los Angeles were emptied. It didn't take long for the Z-Boys to realise that the smooth curves of swimming pool walls were ideal for skating. They used O.J. Simpson's football-shaped pool, as well as a rabbit-shaped one that belonged to a magician. The skaters would get chased away by owners and police, but that only made them more determined. Jay Adams once hired a plane so that he could spot empty pools from above. And many pools didn't even need to be empty: the Z-Boys were known to bring their own pumping equipment to get rid of any remaining water.

The tricks created by the team were awesome. Slides, grinds and lip tricks all became common. And the vertical walls in swimming pools also gave birth to perhaps the most important "leap" in the history of skateboarding tricks: the aerial, where skater and board become airborne. Today a 1080° aerial, in which the skater spins through three full rotations, is the holy grail for many skaters. It was first completed successfully in March 2012 – by a twelve-year-old.

So thanks to the Z-Boys and their swimming pools, the skateboarding world can now enjoy pulling such tricks as "Broken Fingers", "Disaster", "Roast Beef", "Madonna" – and "Sean Penn".

Which if you haven't guessed, is the opposite of a "Madonna".

Chilli Sauce Score:)

WATER FOR ELEPHANTS

(2011, Dir. Francis Lawrence)

The bit where a circus owner fires his workers by throwing them off the train

A white elephant? Given the number of critics who complained about the lack of chemistry between Robert Pattinson and Reese Witherspoon, you might think so. Then again Pattinson – star of the vampiric, navel-gazing angst-fest that is *The Twilight Saga* – isn't exactly known for Pacino-esque displays of on-screen energy and emotion. Actually, *Water for Elephants* is a slice of good, old-fashioned Hollywood storytelling. It helps that the film is set in the handsome surroundings of the 1930s Benzini Circus and contains a mighty performance from co-star Rosie the elephant. But circus life isn't all fun and games, especially with owner Christoph Waltz threatening to "redlight" anyone who crosses him. In the film, redlighting involves throwing an offending employee off the moving circus train. But have there been instances of real-life redlighting?

According to Sara Gruen, on whose book the film is based, yes. Gruen has said that her research into circuses did indeed reveal instances of circus owners firing "someone… by throwing them off the back of a moving train". She then goes on to suggest the etymology of the term redlighting: "The reason it's called redlighting is because – if they like you – they throw you off while the train slows to pass by a railway yard. You can see the red light of the yard and find your way back to town. A courtesy, if you will." The *Oxford English Dictionary* also includes the phrase's definition:

> 1. trans. To force (a thief, tramp, etc.) out of a moving train […]. Hence fig., to discharge or expel; to dispose of, kill. U.S. slang (orig. Circus). – 1919 Billboard 20 Dec. 87/3 The

roughnecks found out that I had some money, and that night I was redlighted off the show. 1927 J. TULLY Circus Parade xvi. 254 The light still gleamed in the open door of the car from which we had been red-lighted.

And there are other mentions of the practice in old circus reports: "…following the sudden Robbins Bros. closing in 1931 which was marred by the 'Redlighting' of the show's workmen from the moving train that night, resulting in the death of one man and injury to several."

So redlighting was for real. But what should you do if you find yourself, as an employee who is surplus to the requirements of the circus, being hauled to the rear carriage of a train and given the old heave-ho? In short, how do you survive being pushed from a train?

Unsurprisingly, the landing is everything. If it's good, it's possible to survive even when the train is chugging along at 110 km/h. And it actually helps to be redlighted and chucked off the *back* of a train – because you're not going to bounce back underneath the wheels. When it comes to the actual moment when body meets ground, try to ensure you're not landing feet first: it's likely you'll break an ankle or leg. Instead cover your head with your arms and try to land as if you're lying stretched flat out. This will help a wider area of your body absorb the impact. Also, you'll probably end up rolling like a log, which is another way of dissipating all that bone-crunching energy. So all there's left to do is to dust yourself down and to think about how to avoid being redlighted in future.

A little less clowning around perhaps?

Chilli Sauce Score:

MOONRAKER

(1979, Dir. Lewis Gilbert)

The bit where Jaws falls out of a plane without a parachute and survives

Metal-mouthed, humungous henchman Jaws (the actor, Richard Kiel is over seven feet tall) has form in the keeping-going-against-all-odds department. Whether it's a building falling on him, a car diving off a cliff and a shark attack in *The Spy Who Loved Me*, or a runaway cable car and falling over a waterfall in *Moonraker*, Jaws could always just dust himself down and carry on. He was never killed off, so he could in theory make another return, although as Kiel is in his seventies now, Jaws probably keeps his steel gnashers in a glass by his bed. But of all his incredible comebacks, surely plummeting from a plane without a parachute was a mishap too far?

First, some (basic) physics. When objects fall in a vacuum they do so at the same rate, no matter their size. But when falling through air, objects – such as 7-foot goons – are subject to the drag caused by air resistance: the heavier an object (especially when it has a small surface area) the less effect the air resistance has, and the faster they will fall until they reach terminal velocity.

Obviously Jaws weighs a great deal – but he also has a large surface area. Velocity is increased if someone falls in a head- or feet-down position. For the henchman's uncontrolled fall in *Moonraker*, we're probably looking at a terminal velocity of around 190 km/h, reached after 12 seconds of falling. Passenger planes fly at around 10,600 metres, meaning that Jaws' descent would have taken about three minutes. He lands on a circus tent, which is supposed to explain his survival. In fact, though, it's not required. Because in reality, many people have survived after falling from planes – even without a big top to break their fall.

Take Irish Guard, Lt Charlie Williams who in Kenya in 2004 fell 1,066 metres headfirst with his feet caught in the cords of his tangled parachute. Lt Williams crashed through the corrugated roof of a hut but emerged with a mere three cracked vertebrae and a dislocated finger. Ten years earlier, Sharon McLelland performed a parachute jump in Ontario, Canada. Her parachute failed to open but she landed in soft dirt and was well enough afterwards to apologise to her instructor for not pulling her reserve. And then there's Joan Murray from the US, whose parachute failed in a jump in 1999. Joan landed in a mound of fire ants, the stings of which are believed to have kept her heart beating.

Even when a parachute fails to deploy properly it will almost always help to slow a person's descent. And the same is true for people known as "wreckage riders", whose aircrafts have been destroyed and who have then fallen with some of the debris, the larger surface area of which has helped to slow them down. For instance, stewardess Vesna Vulović was aboard a Yugoslav DC 9 passenger jet when it exploded in 1972, probably as the result of a bomb. The sole survivor, Vesna fell more than 10,000 m in the wreckage of the plane, before landing in snow. She was initially paralysed but can now walk. Similarly, teenager Juliane Koepcke was in a plane that was stuck by lightning and disintegrated over Peru in 1971. Still strapped into a row of seats (which may have spun round like a sycamore seed, thus reducing its speed), she fell for over 3 kilometres before crashing though the canopy of the Peruvian rainforest. But Juliane survived and, with a broken collarbone and other injuries, she trekked through the forest for over a week before finding help.

But some people don't have the benefit of a faulty parachute or falling wreckage to slow them down. Some people simply fall to earth. Many of these incidents seem to have happened during World War II. One of the most impressive (and scary) involved Nicholas Alkemade, a tail gunner in a Lancaster Bomber. Having been attacked by German fighters, his plane caught fire. But it

wasn't just his plane; it was his parachute too. Preferring to fall rather than burn to death, Nicholas jumped. He fell 5,500m before landing in trees and then snow. And walked away – albeit with a limp from a twisted knee. Just as lucky was Alan Magee, a gunner on a US B-17 which was hit over France in 1943. Alan was thrown from the plane before he could put on his parachute. He fell 6,100m to land on the roof of the St Nazaire train station. His arm was badly injured but he survived to tell the tale.

So if you ever find yourself midair without a plane or parachute, survival is possible. And here are a few tips. If this happens at 10,000 m you'll soon blackout because of a lack of oxygen. So you don't have to worry about anything until you come to again at 4,500 m. Then look around for any large, flat piece of plane to grab hold of and increase your drag, thus decreasing your speed. (If there's nothing to hand, it's time for a bit of D.I.Y. drag, as you spread your body as wide as possible.) Next, head for the trees. It won't hurt if you find a a few branches to crash through... well it will, but you know what I mean. And if the ground's covered in snow, so much the better.

You'll have plucked yourself from the jaws of death.

Chilli Sauce Score: ♪♪

WEAPONRY

"My man is loaded."
Taxi Driver

BABEL

(2006, Dir. Alejandro González Iñárritu)

The bit where Cate Blanchett is shot from a very long way away

 It's not really what you want. You go on holiday to Morocco to patch up your marriage with Brad Pitt. You're bumping along in a tourist bus when, without warning, you're shot through the neck by the son of a goatherd as he tests his father's Winchester M70 to see if it really does have a range of three kilometres.

But is such a long shot in reality... a long shot?

Ever since guns were invented there have been people who have been trained to shoot them a very long way. The riflemen of Louis XIV of France can lay claim to being the first modern snipers, and pretty much made heavy armed cavalry obsolete with their plate armour-piercing lead shot. Later, in 1777, Virginian rifleman Timothy Murphy killed General Simon Fraser of the British Army using his Kentucky rifle from an (at the time) unheard-of distance of 500 metres. The shot turned the battle. And on 9 May 1864, Major General John Sedgwick of the Union Army said of his Confederate enemy 800 metres away, "They couldn't hit an elephant at this distance". A moment later he was shot and killed by a sniper. The most prolific sniper in history is believed to be a Finn, Simo Häyhä. During what has become known as the Winter War, Häyhä shot 542 Soviet soldiers between 30 November 1939 and 6 March 1940, causing a Russian general to comment ruefully, "We gained 57,000 km² of territory. Just enough to bury our dead."

But in terms of quality rather than quantity, no one can beat Corporal Craig Harrison of the Household Cavalry, who in 2009 killed two Taliban machine gunners in Afghanistan from a distance of some 2,500 metres. Corporal Harrison beat the sniping record previously held by a Canadian marksman by 45 m, even though his British-built L115A3 Long Range Rifle was only designed to have a range of 1,500 m. And he was so far away that his bullets took almost three seconds to reach their targets.

It was a long shot but it worked.

Chilli Sauce Score: ♪♪

LIVE AND LET DIE

(1973, Dir. Guy Hamilton)

The bit where a British agent suffers death by sound

Throwing a prosthetic arm out of a train window, Roger Moore ends his first outing as Bond with the words, "Just being disarming, darling". Dodgy pun aside, this line provides a succinct account of Moore's 007 tenure. From not wearing a hat to drinking bourbon instead of martini, "Rog" adds a touch of levity to proceedings. *Live and Let Die* is a rollicking romp through the streets of Harlem and the backwaters of Louisiana to the fictional island of San Monique. It all kicks off with the murder of three British agents who are monitoring the activities of the prime minister of San Monique, Dr Kananga. The first is killed at a meeting of the United Nations in New York when a high-pitched sound is sent through his translation earphones. But is this nefarious deed based on sound principles?

Sonic weapons do exist but tend to be called by the more harmless-sounding term, Long Range Acoustic Devices. And they do have a variety of applications. LRADs have been used by the crew of a luxury cruise liner to deter Somali pirates and by federal authorities to stop looting in New Orleans. Reports have also emerged from post-war Iraq that US troops have access to an LRAD called the Secret Scream, which emits "sonic bullets" that sound like a baby's high-pitched scream. And in 2010, the Scottish Government got into trouble with human rights groups for their failure to ban the "mosquito alarm". This sonic deterrent sends out an irritating high-pitched sound which, because a person's hearing begins to deteriorate when they reach their mid-twenties, can only be heard by people under the age of 25 – a bit like today's chart music.

But how do sonic weapons work and can they kill?

125

Rather than using a single large loudspeaker, LRADs combine many small speakers across a large surface, enabling sound to be transmitted in a focused direction over a distance up to 500 metres. Technically the speakers are 'piezoelectric transducers', which change electrical impulses into sound waves. Identical waves emerge from the each transducer, and their amplitudes combine to create louder sounds. The outer transducers are slightly out of phase with the inner transducers, which cancels out some of the outermost waves. This makes the "beam" of sound more focused, with the volume decreasing by 20 decibels (dB) for every 15 degrees outside the beam. The maximum volume that a LRAD can achieve is 151 dB – compared to 140 dB for a gunshot. A person generally feels pain resulting from sounds over 130 dB and may well suffer damage to their hearing. But it won't kill them. And it doesn't seem difficult to render a LRAD useless: a pair of quality ear-muffs would do the trick.

However, because sound essentially consists of waves of pressure, a big enough sound wave could in theory kill you in the same way that the pressure from a bomb blast can. In World War I, soldiers were often found dead close to the site of an explosion, but without any external injuries. However, there was plenty of damage to their hollow organs, particularly to their ears and lungs. It's thought that the pressure of the blast ruptured their lung tissue, allowing air bubbles to enter their blood and cause fatal embolisms. And it's possible that the same could happen with a very, very loud sound.

So, although a high-pitched sound sent down your earphones is unlikely to give you anything more than a burst eardrum and a nasty headache, that's not to say that sound can't ever kill. Just ask the victims of the inch-long pistol shrimp, a creature that snaps its claw to produce a deafening crack measured at an incredible 218dB. The snapping claw creates a pressure bubble, the internal temperature of which reaches (for a fraction of a second) nearly 4,500°C. When the bubble bursts, it does so with a bang that stuns the shrimp's prey into immobility. It then becomes lunch.

So when it comes to death by sound, forget martinis. You want a shrimp cocktail.

Chilli Sauce Score: ♪♪♪

THE MAN WHO WOULD BE KING

(1975, Dir. John Huston)

The bit where bullets explode in a fire

God's holy trousers! Before Michael Caine and Sean Connery took the parts of Rudyard Kipling's rogue ex-soldiers of the British Raj, John Huston had considered using Clark Gable and Humphrey Bogart, followed by Burt Lancaster and Kirk Douglas, and then Robert Redford and Paul Newman. But it's hard to imagine anyone but Caine and Connery in this very British and thoroughly entertaining tale of derring-do.

At one point, Peachy Carnehan (Caine) ponders: "Now, the problem is how to divide five Afghans from three mules and have two Englishmen left over." His solution is to put a round of ammunition in his mouth and then, having been searched by the tribesmen, to spit it into a campfire where it detonates, distracting the Afghans and allowing Sirs Michael and Sean to overcome them.

But in reality, if a cartridge is put in a fire it will explode with more of a pop than a bang. Certainly not enough to make an Afghan afraid.

For obvious reasons, firefighters have conducted many tests on the effects of fire on ammunition. They have found that they have little to fear. Under normal circumstances (i.e. inside a gun) the propellant in a cartridge burns and creates gases which, under pressure, send the bullet down the barrel. Chuck a cartridge in a fire and there's nothing to contain the pressure when the heat causes the cartridge to rupture (a process called cooking off). With no pressure and no gun barrel, the bullet does little more than drop from its casing. A loaded gun in a fire is a different story. In this instance, cartridges can cook off and then be discharged in a similarly dangerous manner to when the trigger is pulled. And part-time chefs/gun nuts may be interested to know that .22 long rifle cartridges "cook off" at an average of 135°C, .38 Special cartridges at 143°C and 12 gauge shotgun shells at 197°C (Gas Mark 6).

Delia Smith & Wesson, perhaps.

Chilli Sauce Score: ♪♪♪♪♪

THE LAST OF THE MOHICANS

(1992, Dir. Michael Mann)

The bit where Daniel Day-Lewis uses silk to make his rifle shoot further

One of the most talented and enigmatic actors of his generation, Daniel Day-Lewis is renowned for his intensive, some would say obsessive, approach to his work. From learning to box and to skin animals to staying in character throughout the whole production of a film, Day-Lewis' attention to detail has earned him a remarkable number of awards for an actor who has made remarkably few films. But does that attention to detail lapse when it comes to his flintlock rifle?

Day-Lewis is Hawkeye, a white man adopted by the last members of the Mohican tribe of Native Americans. Holed up with a British garrison in Fort William Henry as the French forces attack, Hawkeye helps a messenger to escape from the fort by sniping at the French. As the messenger makes his final dash to the safety of the woods, Hawkeye picks off one last (and very distant) enemy with his rifle, which has been stuffed with a silk patch to create a tighter seal and thus increase its range by forty yards.

The answer, in short, is that a piece of silk might increase the accuracy of a flintlock rifle, but would be unlikely to increase its range. For that purpose, marksmen of the day loaded their rifles with a double charge of gunpowder. More power, more distance. There is, however, one other minor incorrect detail: Hawkeye's rifle didn't exist in the colonial America of 1757.

First developed in the mid 1500s, the flintlock mechanism was the first reliable method of firing a gun. (The "lock" is a gun's ignition mechanism.) Before the flintlock was the matchlock, a slow-burning wick that you would light and then move into position to light the gunpowder. But this took a long time – and God forbid it should rain. The matchlock was strictly for fair-weather combatants only. The flintlock, however, was a great improvement.

The main components of a flintlock are: the hammer, which holds a piece of flint; the mainspring which drives the hammer; a piece of steel called a frizzen that the hammer strikes; and a pan holding a small amount of gunpowder. To fire a flintlock, you'd pour gunpowder down the gun's barrel, wrap a lead bullet in a small bit of cloth (or silk if you're Daniel Day-Hawkeye), place some gunpowder in the pan, snap the frizzen over the pan, cock the hammer and pull the trigger. Simple. The force of the flint striking the steel of the frizzen causes tiny particles of iron to flake off. The friction ignites the iron particles, turning them into sparks and – BANG! However, it's generally thought that rifles didn't appear in Pennsylvania until at least 1760. And the rifle used by Hawkeye in the film is a mixture of several different styles, resembling most of all a southern-style rifle of the 1770s.

So it turns out that *The Last of the Mohicans* isn't quite as accurate as the last of the Mohicans is with his rifle.

Chilli Sauce Score: ♪ ♪ ♪ ♪

POINT BREAK

(1991, Dir. Kathryn Bigelow)

The bit where a petrol pump becomes a flamethrower

A gang of bank robbers called the Ex-Presidents; an orphan surfer girl called Tyler; and Keanu Reeves as (a Hollywood name if ever there was one) Johnny Utah, a rookie FBI agent and former Ohio State quarterback. It should be the ultimate recipe for movie banality. But in the hands of Bigelow, even Reeves gives a surprisingly layered and effective performance. And the action is awesome, dude. But when Bodhi (Patrick Swayze) uses his lighter and a petrol pump to create a makeshift flamethrower...? You cannot be serious!

Makeshift is exactly what the first flamethrowers were when, in the 5th century B.C., burning material such as coal was dropped into a long pipe, then blown out in blowpipe style – a skill it didn't pay to suck at. In the 7th century A.D., things got a bit more sophisticated with the invention of "Greek fire". Although the exact details of its composition have been lost, it's believed that Greek fire was made from a combination of petroleum, sulphur and other ingredients, to produce a highly-flammable liquid. This was transported by Byzantine forces over land and sea and then pumped through narrow brass tubes to produce a powerful jet, ignited by a soldier holding a fuse at the end of the tube.

The invention of guns and gunpowder meant there weren't any significant developments in the world of flamethrowing for the next thousand years or so. During World War I, however, the ability of fire to terrorise and demoralise even the bravest of soldiers was rediscovered. And the perceived iniquity of the flamethrower as a weapon can be judged by the fact that captured flamethrower operators were summarily executed. Apparently, throwing fire at your enemy just wasn't cricket.

In the Second World War, forces on both sides used a range of flamethrowers, from backpack to tank-mounted. The portable flamethrowers usually consisted of two containers holding a flammable, oil-based fuel and a third carrying a compressed gas such as butane. When the trigger was pressed the gas would be forced into the space above the liquid fuel, pushing it under pressure into the gun housing. Here it would flow past an ignition system such as a spark plug, creating a stream of fire that could reach a distance of up to fifty yards.

So in theory, igniting the gasoline as it leaves a petrol pump would be similar to using a flamethrower. In practice, it would be a good idea to reserve a bed in your local burns unit. Pure petrol was rarely used by the military because it was just too flammable. Instead, thickening agents were added to produce a substance that burned slower. One such substance was napalm. A slower burning fuel is more stable, less likely to burn itself out before reaching its target and burns for longer when hitting it. Petrol, on the other hand, tends to go "whoosh!".

This is down to petrol's "flash point", defined as the lowest temperature at which a liquid forms an ignitable mixture with the surrounding air. So it isn't petrol which is dangerously flammable, but its fumes. And petrol's flash point – when fumes are produced – is -43°C (in comparison diesel has a flash point of 62°C or higher). Wherever there's petrol there are likely to be petrol fumes. And wherever there are petrol fumes and a naked flame…

Let's just say Bodhi wouldn't have been going surfing for a while.

Chilli Sauce Score: ♪♪♪♪

THE MAGNIFICENT SEVEN

(1960, Dir. John Sturges)

The bit where James Coburn throws his knife and kills a man

A Hollywood remake of a classic Japanese film would normally be a recipe for cinematic disaster. Yet this really is a magnificent western, with memorable performances from an all-star cast and a classic score by Elmer Bernstein. James Coburn plays Britt, one of seven gunmen hired to protect a Mexican village from bandits. During one of the film's most famous scenes, Britt takes part in a duel and kills his gun-wielding opponent by throwing his switchblade. But is it really possible for a knife thrower to guarantee that it will be their weapon's blade and not its handle that hits the target?

"Ah, that was the greatest shot I've ever seen," another character exclaims after Britt shoots a bandit fleeing on horseback. No, Britt replies, "The worst! I was aiming at the horse." Perhaps it's not surprising he'd want to use a knife instead. But on the face of it, knife-throwing seems to be a rather risky business. With a gun, if you miss you reload and try again. With a knife, if you throw it and it ends up bouncing handle-first off your adversary, not only do you look daft but you're left empty-handed.

As any competitor in a knife-throwing tournament ("darts for real men") will tell you, getting your knife to hit its target tip first is all about practice – practising the same stance, grip – the Side Pinch, Thumb on Top, Bouquet or the Underhand (as used by Coburn) – release and follow-through. Keep your elbow and wrist relaxed and let your arm follow its natural line in one easy movement. And contrary to what you may think, a properly thrown knife doesn't spin countless times in the air. That's when luck rather than skill takes over. A well-thrown large knife will spin through 180° over (roughly) 2-3 metres and through 360° over 3-4 metres. So the other thing that any self-respecting knife-thrower will know is their exact distance from their target. That way they can do the calculations and determine whether their throw will be successful or whether they need to shorten or lengthen their distance to guarantee a hit with the tip.

Back to Britt. He certainly doesn't measure out his distance from his adversary. Getting a tape measure out would have detracted from the drama. But perhaps we can assume that he's participated in many similar confrontations and knows through experience how far away he needs to be standing – though getting the distance wrong by as little as 6 inches can stop a knife from entering its target. But he *is* one of the Magnificent Seven, so we'll give Britt the benefit of the doubt.

However, from a distance that looks to be something like 12 metres, he then chooses to throw his switchblade underarm. Here's the problem: throwing a knife underarm is like throwing a ball underarm. You just don't get the power. And from 12 metres, Britt's switchblade isn't going to embed itself in anything as tough as a cowboy's chest. If you want to see convincing knife-throwing, watch Steven Seagal's blade-wielding chef in *Under Siege*.

And it's not often I find myself using the words "convincing", "Steven" and "Seagal" in the same sentence.

Chilli Sauce Score:))))

THE DAM BUSTERS
(1955, Dir. Michael Anderson)

The bit where bouncing bombs were inspired by Lord Nelson

The destruction of the Death Star in *Star Wars* was inspired by this account of the 1943 RAF operation against the Möhne dams in Germany. (Think about it: the briefing of the crew; the pilots flying through a valley under enemy fire; the ground staff waiting anxiously for news; the need to drop a bomb at a certain distance from the target; an initial failure before ultimate success.) But what about Barnes Wallis and his bouncing bombs? Did he really, as he claims in the film, nick the idea from Horatio Nelson bouncing cannonballs off the sea and into enemy ships?

Sadly there seems to be no direct reference in British naval records to the Vice Admiral engaging in ducks and drakes with cannonballs, with most sources suggesting that he preferred much closer engagement with enemy ships. What Nelson did do, however, was to make sure that his gunners, rather like a Formula 1 pit crew, practised and then practised some more. With HMS Victory able to fire each of its 104 guns every 90 seconds, perhaps the Royal Navy's greatest advantage was the ability of its ships to sustain an unrivalled rate of rapid fire.

But if Wallis didn't get his idea from Nelson in particular, a passage in his real-life writings indicates that he did draw inspiration from the navy. Wallis wrote that "ricochet gunfire was known as early as the 16th century and was used in naval gunnery in the 17th and 18th centuries to extend the effective range."

Cannonballs would indeed bounce if fired from a low trajectory and with the right sea conditions. The problem was that the poor roll stability of naval ships made it impossible to achieve the effect with any consistency. Because of this, gunners were advised to fire

their cannons on rising waves. By doing this, even if their aim was off there was a good chance that the cannonball would plough through the enemy ship's mast and rigging. Firing as the ship fell with the waves could easily result in the cannonball "plugging" harmlessly into the sea.

So bouncing cannonballs were a real, if hard to achieve, phenomenon. A phenomenon, however, which proved to be a smash hit for Barnes Wallis and his men.

Chilli Sauce Score: ♪♪

BLAZING SADDLES

(1974, Dir. Mel Brooks)

The bit where cowboys shoot their guns into the air

 In 2006 the United States Library of Congress selected *Blazing Saddles* for preservation in the National Film Registry, judging it to be "culturally, historically, or aesthetically significant". Not bad for a film whose most famous scene involves a group of bean-fuelled cowboys farting around a campfire. Further lunacy involves a Wild West town where everybody is called Johnson; a man knocking a horse out with a punch; a running Hedy Lamarr joke ("It's *Hedley*"); the whole cast ending up brawling on the Warner Bros. studio lot; and let's not forget cowboys firing their guns into the sky. Didn't they know that what goes up must come down?

One tragic story illustrates just why firing a weapon into the air is illegal in most states in America. It happened over New Year at the beginning of 2010 near Atlanta, Georgia. A four year-old boy called Marquel Peters was attending a church with his family. All of a sudden Marquel collapsed to the floor with a gaping head wound. His distraught parents had no idea what had happened. The little boy was taken to hospital where an x-ray revealed that he had been hit by a bullet. He died soon afterwards.

Further investigation revealed that members of the congregation had heard a popping sound and saw debris falling from the ceiling shortly before Marquel collapsed. And a ballistics expert was quoted as saying that the bullet had most likely come from an AK-47 assault rifle. The police's conclusion was that someone had fired a rifle into the air as part of the New Year celebrations. The bullet had fallen back to earth, through the church roof and into Marquel's skull.

In 1920 the U.S. Army conducted tests to determine the falling speed of bullets fired into the sky from a platform in the middle of a lake. The gun was fixed in position to allow adjustments and a sheet of armour plating was placed over the soldiers firing the gun. Over 500 shots were fired but, owing to wind, only four bullets fell back down to strike the platform. When the bullets were fired into the sky they decelerated immediately from 820 metres per second because of gravity and air drag, until they momentarily stopped at a height of 2.7 kilometres before falling back down to earth. The bullets then accelerated until they reached terminal velocity, which is when the drag caused by the air equals the pull of gravity, something that is determined by an object's shape and density. Feathers have a terminal velocity of a couple of feet per second. The tests showed that .30 calibre bullets fall somewhat faster, at around 90 metres per second – or 320km/h.

For the 150-gram bullets, this corresponded to 40 joules of energy. Yet earlier tests had shown that a bullet required an average of 80 joules of energy to be lethal.

However, tell that to Marquel.

Chilli Sauce Score: ♪♪♪

TAXI DRIVER

(1976, Dir. Martin Scorsese)

The bit where a gun dealer says that a .44 Magnum can kill an elephant

The film that was not only inspired by real-life would-be assassin, Arthur Bremer, but which in turn went on to inspire the man who shot Ronald Reagan, John Hinckley Jr. Robert De Niro plays Vietnam veteran turned cab driver turned murderous vigilante, Travis Bickle. "Are you looking at me?" No sir, especially as you're sporting some serious firepower and a very scary mohican. Bickle is buying a mini-arsenal of handguns. Gun dealer Easy Andy runs through the benefits of each weapon. When he comes to the .44 Magnum, he says it's powerful enough to kill an elephant. If you've seen *Dirty Harry*, you'll know all about the stopping power of this formidable gun. But could it really bring down the world's largest land animal?

First, let's get one thing straight: there's no such weapon as the .44 Magnum. The .44 refers to the cartridge and its full name is the .44 Remington Magnum. The six-shot, double-action revolver as used by Travis and 'Dirty' Harry Callaghan is actually the Smith & Wesson Model 29. The cartridge's predecessor was the .357 Magnum, which was used in the hunting of antelope, deer and even bears. The .44-calibre cartridge was developed in the 1950s with seriously enhanced killing power. It propels a 240-grain bullet (a grain is a unit of measurement equalling 1/7000 of a pound) at over 450m/sec with 1,750 joules of energy. That's double the force of the .357 and three times as much as a .45 Colt. Once the bullet had been developed, there was then the need to build a gun that could handle it. Hence the Smith & Wesson Model 29. With a bigger cylinder, heavier 16.5cm barrel, wider trigger and larger grips, it's a serious weapon with a serious kick; and it's capable of slaying some pretty serious beasts.

But it's not just the cartridge and the gun that determine stopping-power; the bullet does too. Even with a .44 Magnum cartridge and a Model 29 weapon, many bullets are only "good" for deer and antelope. However, load a 320-grain SSK .44 FP bullet and your handgun will be ready to take on anything from buffalo to bulls and, yes, bull elephants. Because, until ivory hunting was banned, elephants were indeed slaughtered by handgun-wielding hunters. Slow, heavy bullets would often be used, as they wouldn't fragment inside the animal but would pass straight through. (One of the heaviest hunting rounds today, the solid brass .600 Overkill, when loaded into a rifle, will penetrate six feet of oak.) The result would be that, if it wasn't killed instantly, the elephant would leave a blood trail which could be followed.

So yes a .44 Magnum can kill an elephant. Or rather the nut wielding it can.

Chilli Sauce Score: ⟩

BULLITT

(1968, Dir. Peter Yates)

The bit where a man is blasted backwards by a shotgun

The title makes this film sound like it should be completely about guns. But it's the cars that are the stars, namely a green 1968 Ford Mustang GT CID Fastback and a black 1968 Dodge Charger R/T 440 Magnum. Steve McQueen chases two hitmen up and down the steep streets of San Francisco in the best-remembered car chase in film history. And then there's some other stuff about a politician and the mafia (as well as the first use of the word "bullsh*t" in a major film). The chase occurs because one of the hitmen has shot a man in protective custody with a pump-action shotgun. The hit happens in a hotel room and the victim, a supposed mob informant, flies backwards because of the force of the blast.

It's a bloody and dramatic moment, but unfortunately the law of conservation of momentum also renders it highly unlikely.

Conservation of momentum was derived by Sir Isaac Newton from his laws of motion, which were first published in his *Philosophiæ Naturalis Principia Mathematica* of 1687. These laws explained the motion of physical objects, and the third of them states that, "To every action there is always opposed an equal reaction: or the mutual actions of two bodies upon each other are always equal, and directed to contrary parts. Whatever draws or presses another is as much drawn or pressed by that other. If you press a stone with your finger, the finger is also pressed by the stone."

This equates to the conservation of momentum. Momentum refers to the mass of an object multiplied by its velocity and it is always conserved, even in collisions. The shot from the shotgun may have a very high velocity, but its mass, when compared to

an adult human, is negligible. So, therefore, is the chance of the victim being thrown backwards after having been hit. Moreover, bullets, when fired from close range, often pass straight through a victim and thus conserve some of the momentum themselves without transferring it to the person's body.

Momentum is different from energy. Kinetic energy is defined as the work required to accelerate an object from rest. And this type of energy is not conserved in a collision, including when a bullet hits somebody. Instead the energy is transferred to flesh and bone, blood and guts. It is this kinetic energy that filmmakers pretend will knock a person back fifteen feet against a wall. (This is not to say that the idea of "knockback" hasn't been promoted by real ballistics manufacturers too. Heavy "Manstopper" bullets have been used by various forces and organisations because of their supposed ability to stop attackers in their tracks.) Yet even a .44 Magnum is simply incapable of stopping a running person's forward momentum.

However, a type of "knockback" does exist and has been witnessed in real-life shootings. It's nothing to do with the force of the bullets. Instead it's an innate human response to being hit. A person who is struck by a fist or a bullet is conditioned to absorb the blow by moving with the force i.e. backwards. But flying through the air just doesn't happen.

In fact, it's bullsh*t.

Chilli Sauce Score: ♩♩♩♩

LICENCE TO KILL

(1989, Dir. John Glen)

The bit where Bond is beaten up by ninjas

Think of all the tough nuts that Bond has beaten to a pulp over the years. From Robert Shaw's hard-as-nails Red Grant in *From Russia with Love*, through chuckling, one-armed Tee Hee in *Live and Let Die*, to turncoat Alec Trevelyan in *Goldeneye*. Yet when Timothy Dalton comes up against two undercover narcotics agents dressed as ninjas, he's overcome quicker than you can say "What an uninspiring title for a Bond movie". Is the legendary ninja the ultimate combatant? Or just the stuff of legends?

Japanese folklore suggests that ninjas are descended from a demon that was half man, half crow, which would suggest that the silent assassins are more myth than mortal. But ninjas are found in history as well as storybooks. The word comes from the Japanese *shinobi-no-mono*, which is written with two kanji characters that can also be pronounced "nin-sha" – the first character, *nin*, suggests stealth while the second denotes a person. The collective term for the ninja's combat skills is ninjutsu.

Most sources suggest that the skills that became ninjutsu were developed in Japan between 600 and 900 A.D. By the year 850, the Chinese Tang Dynasty was on its last legs and some Tang generals escaped to Japan, taking their battle know-how with them. They were followed in the 11th century by Chinese monks who brought their own combat philosophies, many of which had originated in India. These tactics found a natural affinity with the systems of self-improvement that were being developed in Japan at that time, including the practices of the mountain-dwelling Shugenja, who sought enlightenment by exposing themselves to the elements.

The resulting code wasn't formalised until the 12th century when a defeated samurai, Daisuke Togakure, bumped into a Chinese warrior monk, Kain Doshi, whilst wandering the mountains of southwest Honshu. Daisuke renounced the samurai code of bushido and he and Doshi developed the new underground code of ninjutsu. And this really sums up what ninjas are about: they're about anything that samurai are not. Samurai were hired by the ruling elite and valued loyalty and honour. They wore bright colours to display their clan identity and in battle they would select a single opponent, announce their challenge and list their family pedigree, all before attacking (assuming their opponent hadn't got bored of waiting and gone home). By contrast the ninjustu code was developed in reaction to the power of the feudal aristocracy. By its very nature, peasant resistance needed to be much more secretive than the way of the samurai, and limited resources led to the use of whatever weapons and means were readily accessible. So poisoning, seduction, spying and general sneakiness were all considered fair play.

At some stage, ninjas began to be organised into families. Fighters were probably trained from childhood, and women certainly served as ninjas, often disguising themselves as dancers and concubines to infiltrate enemy castles. Such was the ninjas' effectiveness that they began to be hired by the samurai themselves to do the dirty work that their bushido code prevented. In terms of ninja clothing, the blue outfits worn in *Licence to Kill* are fairly accurate. Most movie ninjas are dressed to kill in black but this comes from theatrical representations. Real-life ninjas were more likely to wear dark blue for night operations, and clothing that blended in with their surroundings for the rest of the time.

Ninja tools and weapons often had agricultural origins, owing to the peasant backgrounds of many of the fighters. So modified sickles, saws and shears were used – having the advantage that they wouldn't betray a ninja's intentions if discovered. (The weapon of choice for every bedroom martial artist, the *nunchaku*,

actually began life as a rice thresher.) Special equipment was also developed, including the *shuko* (an iron hand-crampon used for climbing) and the *tessen* (a sharpened metal fan). Some ninjas disguised themselves as flute-playing performers – their instruments serving as handy blow-dart tubes. Opinions differ as to whether ninjas ever used throwing stars. If they did, the stars were most likely used as a means of distraction, as their size was unlikely to make them deadly. Other rumoured devices included footwear with animal tracks on the soles, folding boats and air-filled shoes to enable walking on water.

It has been suggested that the amount of equipment ninjas were supposed to have carried would have precluded them from going anywhere with the slightest degree of stealth. However each ninja would have had only one or two specialities – and in any case, ninjutsu was always much more than just violent combat. Concealment, toxicology, climbing, fire and water, the use of deadly pressure points on an enemy's body, astronomy, survival, navigation and medicine were all used by the ninja families.

And then there was magic – or rather, good P.R. The myth of the flying, invisible ninjas who could pass through walls arose because castle guards couldn't work out how anyone could climb up a vertical wall before killing their victim without leaving a mark. The answer would be crampons and poison, but to the uninitiated (and terrified) it smacked of the supernatural. And so the ninjas' reputation for super-human abilities was enhanced.

The Edo Period (1603-1868) brought stability and peace to Japan and the ninja story to a close. Apart, that is, from in the cinema, where the legend of the ninjas is definitely alive – and kicking.

Chilli Sauce Score: 🌶

JOHNNY DANGEROUSLY

(1984, Dir. Amy Heckerling)

The bit where a falling bomb makes a whistling sound

Dom DeLuise appearing as the Pope: it should be enough to put anyone off this gangster spoof. But, even though it begins to misfire towards the end, the film scores more hits than misses. It's also one of the first films to have been given a PG-13 rating, no doubt thanks to baddie Roman Moronie's habit of mispronouncing swearwords: "You lousy cork-soakers," "Fargin iceholes" and "This somanabatch" being amongst his juiciest. Michael Keaton plays the eponymous hero, who turns to a life of crime to pay for his neurotic mother's medical bills. One incident involves Johnny blowing up Moronie's nightclub with a bomb dropped from a biplane. The bomb whistles on the way down. Has it forgotten the words to a song? Or is the director suggesting that this is what happens in real life?

Of course, it isn't the bombs themselves that whistle but the air rushing past them. The imperfect shapes of early 20th-century bombs and the attached stabilizing fins meant that the high velocity air currents produced as they fell really did produce a variety of screams, shrieks and whistles. Indeed the German newspaper, *Der Adler,* carried an article in 1942 which stated:

> One question that we often hear posed is: If I can hear a bomb whistling, does that mean it is going to hit me? Front-line soldiers have found that when they hear bullets whistle, the bullets do not hit them because by that time they have already flown past. Often people take this fact and try to apply it to aerial bombs. The answer is that bombs tend to fall slower than bullets fly. As long as the bomb is falling at a rate below the speed of sound, its whistling will precede it and will be audible at its place of impact.

Nowadays, bombs are far more aerodynamic and consequently far quieter. But in World War II – and even later – the average explosive dropped from a bomber was little more than a drum filled with high explosives. The British called them "cookies", and their shape created a good deal of wind noise. It was a sound that could have an extreme psychological effect on those on the ground: even if you weren't blown to pieces in an aerial bombardment the screams of the falling explosives were likely to give you nightmares. Of course the Nazis were quick to take advantage of the terror with one of the most infamous Luftwaffe aircraft of World War II.

Stuka (from Sturzkampfflugzeug, meaning dive bomber) referred to any German bomber. But the term was really owned by the Junkers Ju 87, which destroyed more ships than any other aircraft, and was second in the list for tanks. The Ju 87 carried one 250 kg bomb (later increased to 500 kg) under its fuselage, four 50 kilo bombs under its wings and dived at a stomach-churning, heart-stopping angle of almost 90 degrees. These bombs were occasionally fitted with tube-shaped whistles to add to the terror of the enemy below. And some planes were even fitted with a device called a "Jericho siren", which created and amplified a wailing sound when the Ju 87s dived.

So films which use whistling bombs are fairly accurate – except when, as in *Johnny Dangerously,* they show the bomb falling from a ground camera position, and with a whistle that *descends* in pitch. Because the pitch should actually rise, as predicted by the Doppler shift, first explained in 1842 by the Austrian, Christian Doppler. Doppler discovered that sound is made up of waves of high and low pressure (the distance between the wave crests is the sound's wavelength). If the source of a sound (such as a whistling 500 kg bomb) is moving towards you, you get exposed to more pressure variations per second and that equates to the perception of a rising pitch. (Of course if a falling bomb were shown from inside a plane – rather than from the ground – the whistling

should indeed descend in pitch, as the Doppler shift also works negatively.) But falling bombs with a rising pitch just wouldn't feel right: we naturally expect descending things to be accompanied by a sound that descends rather than rises in pitch.

Sorry to break this bombshell, but that's just not what happens.

Chilli Sauce Score: 🌶🌶

FOOD AND DRINK

"The carrot has mystery."
Withnail and I

THE GREAT ESCAPE

(1963, Dir. John Sturges)

The bit where alcohol is distilled from potatoes

This perennial bank holiday classic – Steve McQueen's third movie to appear in this these pages – sees him as "Cooler King" Captain Hilts. In reality only a Dutchman and two Norwegians managed to flee successfully from Stalag Luft III POW camp and not a single American participated in the escape. So obviously the scene in which Hilts and his compatriots celebrate Independence Day by brewing moonshine from a sackful of spuds didn't really happen. But can it be done?

It can and it is, although it's illegal to distill spirits in the UK without the appropriate licence. Here's how you do it. The first stage is to boil and mash your potatoes so as to gelatinize (break down) the starch they contain; a pressure cooker (or a cobbled-together version of one, as in the film) is ideal for this. Next the gelatinized starch must be converted into sugar, a process called saccharification. Commercial distillers use enzymes – proteins that increase the rate of chemical reaction – to do this. The home or POW-camp distiller can get the same effect using cereal grains which have been malted (a process in which the grains are prompted to develop enzymes by being soaked in water to make them germinate, then dried with hot air to prevent further germination). The malted cereal is then added, and the resultant mixture held at 70ºC for two hours, during whihc time the starch molecule is converted into simple sugars like maltose.

The next stage is to ferment the sugars using yeast. It's quite conceivable that Hilts and his fellows would have been able to get hold of some baker's yeast, seeing as one of them – Hendley the Scrounger (James Garner) – seemed able to procure pretty much anything, from a camera to acres of fabric. Alternatively, wild yeast

could have been used, although the results tend to be much more hit-and-miss. After the fermentation process, what you're left with is a potato "wine" of 6-8% ABV (alcohol by volume). So far so perfectly legal, by the way – just not very nice to drink.

The final – less legal – stage is distillation. This process, which has been used for over a thousand years, takes advantage of the fact that at just under 80°C alcohol has a lower boiling point than water. By gently heating the wine, the alcohol evaporates and the vapour can then be condensed and collected. Commercial distillers complete the whole process in a fixed still, which can be heated and then cooled. Alternative distillation equipment can be as simple as a kettle with a hosepipe attached to the spout. The alcohol vapour collects in the hose which is immersed in a bucket of cold water to enable the vapour to condense. The resulting spirit is then drained into another bucket. If you ever find yourself in Mongolia, you may well see a goatskin being used in which tribesmen heat fermented yak milk before burying it in snow to condense the alcohol vapour. Delicious, I'm told.

By redistilling the liquid, it's possible to bump the ABV up to 40%. However the spirit produced isn't vodka as defined by today's law. It's closer to poitín (anglicised as poteen or potcheen), an Irish spirit which, with an ABV of 60%-90%, is one of the strongest drinks in the world. In fact some people have been known to get intoxicated a second time the morning after drinking poitín, merely by drinking a glass of water and thus bringing the leftover ethanol in their body back into solution.

No wonder Harry ended up twenty feet short.

Chilli Sauce Score:

WITHNAIL AND I

(1986, Dir. Bruce Robinson)

The bit where Withnail drinks lighter fluid

Of course if you can't get hold of any potatoes you could always try ligh… No don't even think about it. And if you are thinking about it, read the section below. You have been warned!

Set in 1969, *Withnail and I* is basically a homage to getting off your head – making Richard E. Grant's casting as Withnail both surprising and inspired, seeing as he was a teetotaller who had never been drunk. The film has even spawned a drinking game where viewers try to match the on-screen imbibing measure for measure. But there's one beverage they won't be having.

Withnail, having emptied his Camden flat of conventional alcohol, resorts to pouring lighter fluid down his throat. During filming, director Bruce Robinson had the water in the lighter fluid bottle swapped with vinegar for the actual take. So Grant's gagging is for real. But what would happen if you really were imbecilic enough to drink lighter fluid?

Benzene, butane, hexamine, lacolene, naptha and propane may all be found in lighter fluid, depending on the brand. And they're all toxic. In some cases where lighter fluid has been poured directly into the throat, instant death has occurred because the sudden and extreme toxicity has caused the body to flood the lungs with fluid. However even if sudden death is avoided, the ingestion of lighter fluid tends to result in a host of other symptoms that make sudden death seem like a better idea. Loss of vision; severe pain in the throat; severe pain or burning in the nose, eyes, ears, lips, or tongue; burns to the oesophagus; damage to the gastrointestinal lining; blood in the vomit; blood in the stool; low blood pressure; breathing difficulties; dizziness; extreme sleepiness; necrosis

of skin and tissues; coma. And these symptoms can continue for weeks after the fluid – for fluid read poison – was ingested.

If you do happen upon someone who, instead of investing money and time this book, has spent their money on lighter fluid and their time drinking it, seek immediate medical attention. Do not make them throw up unless instructed to do so by a healthcare professional. Give them water or milk unless vomiting, convulsions or a decreased level of alertness make it difficult for them to swallow.

If only proper medical aid had been given to the man who was the inspiration for Withnail: an aristocratic, alcoholic, out-of-work and out-of-control actor called Vivian MacKerrell. The lighter fluid scene is based on something that MacKerrell actually did. He couldn't see for days afterwards and Robinson suspects that the throat cancer that eventually killed his friend was caused by the incident.

"I feel like a pig shat in my head," says Withnail. You should be so lucky.

Chilli Sauce Score: ♪♪♪♪

ON HER MAJESTY'S SECRET SERVICE

(1969, Dir. Peter R. Hunt)

The bit where Bond knows his caviar

 Poor George Lazenby. Okay, so unlike Roger Moore he never had to cook a quiche on screen (in a scene in *A View To A Kill*, which saw Moore become spokesman for the British Quiche Council). Yet Lazenby remains the odd-one-out of the Bond stars. By general consensus, he failed to fill Connery's shoes. (Has anyone succeeded?) But *OHMSS* is a bona fide Bond classic: brilliantly directed, memorably scored – and Lazenby ain't half bad, displaying a more human side to Bond. Plus, he knows his Beluga from his Sevruga, as he identifies the former when tucking into some caviar shortly after dispatching a hotel room-breaking henchman. But what's the difference?

Caviar refers to the salted roe of the sturgeon. The vast majority of caviar consumed around the world comes from the Caspian Sea, which is surrounded by Russia, Kazakhstan, Turkmenistan, Iran and Azerbaijan, and is in fact not a sea but the world's largest lake. Roe from only three of the twenty-six species of sturgeon in the Caspian – the Sevruga, Osetra and Beluga – are used for caviar. It's estimated that stocks in the Caspian Sea fell by up to 90% in the early 1990s because of over-fishing. Today, trade is strictly controlled by the United Nations.

The sevruga is the most abundant sturgeon species in the Caspian Sea. It matures in five to seven years and its roe are the smallest in size, their colour ranging from light to dark grey. They are also the creamiest and strongest in flavour. It was the favourite caviar of Charles de Gaulle. Ian Fleming preferred his caviar from the Osetra sturgeon, which reaches maturity after between twelve and fifteen years. Ranging from golden yellow to brown in colour, Osetra caviar has medium-sized roe and a fruity, nutty flavour.

The most expensive caviar comes from the Beluga sturgeon, which is the rarest of the Caspian species. It takes the Beluga at least twenty years to reach egg-producing maturity. The Beluga is also the largest of the sturgeon, weighing up to 1,800 pounds, reaching 20 feet and over 100 years of age. Favoured by Pablo Picasso, Beluga has the largest roe, with a grey colour and a delicate, slightly buttery flavour. Each sturgeon species produces caviar with its own distinct flavour, and none is universally considered superior to the others. But the most prized is a variety called Almas caviar (meaning 'diamond' in Persian). Almas is pearly white in colour and comes from older Beluga sturgeons between sixty and eighty years old. It sells for as much as $25,000 per kilogram.

So now you know as much about caviar types as James Bond, how should you serve it? It's simple: simply. The classic way of serving caviar is in its jar or tin, nestling in a large shallow bowl of crushed ice. A spoon made from mother-of-pearl or bone is traditionally provided (sterling silver spoons give the roe a metallic taste). Caviar can be accompanied with plain toast or, if you're really daring, new potatoes or blinis with crème fraiche. When using toast, purists (and size zero supermodels) tend not to eat the toast, but simply scrape the caviar off it with their teeth. In terms of liquid refreshment, caviar is often taken with chilled vodka or – Bond's preference – brut (dry) champagne.

So it may have been Moore 7 – Lazenby 1 in terms of Bond appearances. But it's definitely 1-0 to George in the taste test.

Chilli Sauce Score: ♪

NATIONAL LAMPOON'S ANIMAL HOUSE

(1978, Dir. John Landis)

The bit where John Belushi eats a golf ball

The film that launched a thousand toga parties. It's a riot/orgy/road-trip/food-fight from beginning to end. Delta Tau Chi is the Faber College frat house where anything goes, as long as it goes with a bang. And Belushi is Bluto, master of mayhem, flunker of exams, decimator of guitars and, yes, consumer of golf balls. A ball has been hit into the campus kitchens, landing in a pot of soup. It's not long before Belushi is hoovering up everything there is to eat in the student cafeteria, including a bowl of soup containing the ball, on which our hero munches quite happily. But surely this scene is hard to swallow?

Today's golf balls use a variety of different materials for their outer layers – materials which have in common the quality of hardness. Surlyn, the trade name for a thermoplastic resin, is one of the most popular and durable contemporary cover materials. But in the '60s when the film was set (and in the '70s when it was shot) a substance called balata was often used.

What's under the cover is also relevant. The two-piece golf balls used by most ordinary golfers are undeniably difficult to eat. These are made from a solid core of acrylate or resin, and are then covered in surlyn. Three-piece golf balls, however, have a rubber or liquid core with metres of elastic wound round it. Wound balls are softer and so give skilful players more control. They also won't leave you with quite so many broken teeth.

The hardness of a golf ball is known as its "compression" and each ball is given a rating between 0 and 200. This number indicates how much the ball changes its shape (compresses) when

it is subjected to a force. A ball that doesn't compress is rated 200. For every 1/1000th of an inch that a ball does compress, it drops one point until a ball that compresses 2/10ths of an inch or more is rated zero.

So we need a three-piece, balata-coated ball, preferably with a compression rating of about -5000. But if golf balls are anything like meat (who am I kidding?) then they'll benefit from a bit of cooking. It's the amount of collagen in a cut of meat that determines how long it needs to be cooked before becoming tender – the more collagen, the longer the cooking time. Weight-bearing muscles, such as those in a cow's legs, chest and rump, contain more collagen and need longer in the pot. Collagen is actually a long protein and is shaped in a similar way to how fibres are twisted round each other to form rope. It's this that gives collagen its strength. One can imagine that with twenty metres of elastic twisted round its core, a three-piece golf ball is going to require a few months of stewing to get it anywhere near tender.

So it's not looking good for Bluto. But wait, the film's called *Animal House*. Delta Tau Chi's members act like animals. Perhaps they can eat like them too. Perhaps they can eat like Oscar, a five year-old Labrador from Scotland, who in 2008 was taken to the vet after his owner noticed a rattling noise coming from his stomach. One operation later and thirteen golf balls had been removed from Oscar, who was thought to have swallowed them when on walkies near the local golf course.

Nevertheless, the idea that a human (even one as bestial as Bluto) could bite, chew and swallow a golf ball really does need to be taken with a massive pinch of salt.

Chilli Sauce Score:

DUMB AND DUMBER

(1994, Dir. Peter and Bobby Farrelly)

The bit where chillis kill a criminal

Two directors and, in Jim Carrey and Jeff Daniels, two complete idiots. Jim and Jeff are Lloyd Christmas and Harry Dunne: dumb and dumber, or is it dumber and dumb. It's slapstick and gross-out comedy at its most uproarious; if you drink something while watching the film, your drink *will* end up coming out your nose. Lloyd and Harry are on their way to Aspen when they stop off at Dante's diner, the "Hottest Food East of the Mississippi". Having themselves suffered the consequences of eating some very hot chilli peppers, they then load the burger of one of the thugs who is chasing them with extra chillis as a joke. It's a prank that ends in his death.

Can chillis (or indeed chilli sauce) really kill? There are about 25 species of chilli in the genus Capsicum, which range from mild and sweet to hot and pungent. Chillis originated in Central and South America, where there is evidence that they were consumed as early as 7500 B.C. The world's largest producer of chillis today is India, where they are also the cheapest available vegetable and, therefore, consumed by many on a daily basis. They also play a part in many Indian superstitions, such as the custom of hanging chillis and lemon over the doorway of your home to deter evil spirits.

But why are chillis anything but chilly? It's believed that they produce the capsaicin (which produces the burning sensation) so that they don't get eaten by mammals (apart from idiotic ones like the human being). In contrast, birds, which help with the dispersal of the chilli's seeds, are not affected by the chilli's heat. Although many people believe it's the seeds that are hot, the capsaicin is actually in the chilli's membranes. Similarly, size

doesn't matter: the myth that smaller chillis are hotter is just that. But the sensation that chillis are "hot" is not. Capsaicin allows calcium ions to enter into our cell membranes. These then trigger pain signals, the same that are sent when cells are exposed to heat. Yet paradoxically, exposure to capsaicin decreases a person's sensitivity to pain. And as a result, it's used as a counter-irritant in the treatment of conditions such as arthritis.

One way of measuring the heat factor of chillis is with Scoville Heat Units. In 1912, American chemist Wilbur Scoville developed a test in which ground chillis were blended with sugar-water. The mixture was then sipped by testers before being increasingly diluted until a point when the testers could no longer taste the heat of the chillis. Each chilli was then given a score depending on how many dilutions were required. Sweet bell peppers have a rating of zero Scoville units, but then they rarely lead to screen villains' deaths. How about the Naga Jolokia (ghost pepper) with a Scoville rating of 1,041,427? Consider that one part of chilli heat per 1,000,000 drops of water is rated at only 1.5 Scoville units. Consider that the hottest chilli normally available, the habanero, has a rating of "only" a few hundred thousand. Consider taking out a life insurance policy before even thinking about eating one. One fool who ate a Naga Jolokia has been quoted (presumably by the paramedics) as saying, "It is so hot you can't even imagine. When you eat it, it's like dying."

And people do occasionally die. A 33-year-old forklift driver from Doncaster called Andrew Lee, a self-confesssed "chilli head", consumed a plate of hot chilli sauce he'd made himself. Later that night he began itching all over. The next morning his girlfriend found him dead on the floor. The cause of death was recorded as heart failure, and a similar reaction has been witnessed in rats which have keeled over in shock having been exposed to high levels of capsaicin.

If you do find that your head's in danger of exploding after you've chewed on an extra hot chilli, don't bother downing ten

litres of water: capsaicin is only soluble in fats and alcohol. But before you get over-excited, beer and wine don't contain enough alcohol to be effective. So grab yourself a pint of milk.

And make sure you're extremely careful what you touch the next time you visit the lavatory.

Chilli Sauce Score: 𝄐

A FUNNY THING HAPPENED ON THE WAY TO THE FORUM

(1966, Dir. Richard Lester)

The bit where Pseudolus asks whether 1 was a good year for wine

A hero played by a man named Zero; Frank Spencer playing a man called Hero; and a terminally-ill Buster Keaton in his very last film. This musical comedy set in ancient Rome is a hit-and-miss mish-mash of familiar faces, fast-paced jokes, buxom beauties, lascivious men and Stephen Sondheim's great songs. Broadway favourite Zero Mostel reprises his stage role as Pseudolus the slave, attempting to win his freedom by helping his young master (Michael Crawford) win the heart of the girl next door. The film certainly looks authentically Roman, but when Pseudolus asks of the wine, "Was 1 a good year?", is it inaccurate as well as funny?

Romans were indeed familiar with wine vintages, but for much of ancient Rome's history it was Greek wine that was the favoured choice for connoisseurs. Romans tended to prefer beer or mead and would send the wine they produced to the Gauls, who were more than a little partial. But when they sacked Carthage in 146 B.C., the Romans got their hands on what is thought to have been the first book ever written about winemaking, and a few years later Cato wrote his *De Agri Cultura* on matters agri- and viticultural. And Roman winemakers never looked back.

So what did the Romans do for us, wine-wise? Well, apart from classifying many varieties of grape and inventing the wooden wine barrel, they were also the first to use glass wine bottles (although instead of using corks they floated a layer of olive oil on the wine). And they perfected the art of getting drunk. The Greeks were fond of philosophising over a jug of wine. But the

Romans took partying to a whole new level, incorporating dancing girls, orgies and getting monumentally smashed. Wine also played an important part in religious ceremonies and was poured down specially designed holes in tombs so that the dead could share a glass with the living.

The idea that some vineyards deserve special recognition, as with today's *Premier Cru* wines, originated in the second century B.C., and among the first such outfits were the Roman vineyards known as Falernian, Alban and Caecuban. As wine production became more sophisticated, its consumption became more impressive. At one time it was estimated that the people of Rome alone were drinking their way through over 47 million gallons each year – an average of one pint of wine a day for every citizen (including children). As a wine's origin was important, so too was its year. For instance, 121 B.C. was thought to have provided the perfect wine-making conditions, and resulted in a legendary Falernian vintage, which was still being drunk over a century later.

But was 1 A.D. a good year? There's no mention of it being so. Besides, there's a more fundamental issue. The Christian Anno Domini chronology wasn't formulated until the 6th century A.D., when a monk called Dionysius Exiguus was commissioned by Pope John I to work out a new calendar. Previously the Romans had used A.U.C., which stands for *Ab urbe condita*, meaning "from the founding of the City". Exiguus calculated that Jesus Christ had been born in the year 753 A.U.C. – so 1 A.D. in his new system would have begun on 1st January 754 A.U.C. However, to complicate matters still further, the most common way Romans of the time referred to a year was to use the names of the two consuls who were serving. So Pseudolus should actually have asked, "Was the consulship of Gaius Caesar and Aemilius Paullus a good year?"

It's enough to drive one to drink.

Chilli Sauce Score: ♪♪♪

COCKTAIL

(1988, Dir. Roger Donaldson)

The bit where a Red Eye is the best cure for a hangover

After all that Roman wine, you may need something to help you through the morning after. And who better to ask than Doug Coughlin (played by Bryan Brown), bartender extraordinaire and part-time philosopher? Tom Cruise is his cocktail-shaking protégé in this eighties cheese-fest, which seems to be loved and derided in equal measure. But is lager, vodka and tomato juice mixed with a raw egg really the best way to get rid of the aches and the shakes?

Let's start with the basics: what is a hangover? If it was a single thing, there's no doubt an effective cure would have been developed. But the word hangover covers a multitude of symptoms. The main after-effect of drinking is dehydration. Alcohol is a diuretic, as anyone knows who has had a beer or two. It affects the pituitary gland in the brain and stops vasopressin being produced, which is a hormone that usually signals the kidneys to reabsorb water. With no vasopressin on tap, water goes straight into the bladder which fills up and then needs to be emptied… again and again and again. When the body's organs find they don't have enough water they begin to siphon it off from anywhere they can, including the brain's cells. This causes the brain to shrink and the filaments connecting its outside membranes to the inside of the skull to stretch. The result is a headache. (The brain itself can't feel pain.)

With the loss of water comes a drop in the body's salt level. Potassium and sodium ions help nerves and muscles to function, and a deficit can cause nausea and aching. Alcohol also attacks the body's stores of glycogen, lowering blood sugar levels and causing a drop in energy. Finally, during the liver's battle with the booze, a large amount of unstable molecules called free radicals

are produced. These are usually taken care of by an enzyme called glutathione but, when reserves run low, the free radicals remain free to cause further damage to the liver.

So that's a hangover. But what about a cure? A strong cup of coffee is a perennial favourite. And yes, the caffeine will perk your body and mind up, but it's not actually curing you. And, like alcohol, caffeine is a diuretic and will cause you to lose even more water. In this respect, soluble vitamin tablets, stomach settler powders and isotonic sports drinks can help, because – as well as replacing lost sugars, salts and vitamins – they also help to bump water levels back up. A hot shower, especially on the back of the neck, may help to relax the tense neck muscles and constricted blood vessels that can cause headaches. Likewise, a walk in the fresh air will increase oxygen intake and improve your metabolic rate, helping to speed up the elimination of poisons. Some swear by an amino acid supplement sold in health food shops called N-acetyl-cysteine, which is extremely good at combating free radicals. Whereas others believe that a hair of the dog is the only way. These last actually have a point, because the liver first breaks down the ethanol in the alcohol before moving on to the methanol, the latter releasing formic acid which makes you feel queasy. By topping up on alcohol the liver has to start again on the ethanol, putting off the processing of methanol and the release of formic acid. However, the words "delaying" and "inevitable" do spring to mind.

In terms of food, a good old bacon sarnie can help on two fronts. The carbohydrates in the bread can help speed up your metabolism and the breaking down of the alcohol. And bacon, as well as being salty, is full of the amino acids that make up protein and can help to restore the neurotransmitters in your sore head. Which brings us to eggs. We've already seen how the ingredients of Doug Coughlin's Red Eye might help to soften the blow of the mother of all hangovers: the tomato juice containing sugars, salts and vitamins, the alcohol acting as the hair of the dog. However the magic ingredient may well be the raw egg. Chicken eggs are one of nature's marvels, full of protein, vitamins and minerals. And to top it all off, they also contain cystelline which, as you will remember, is very effective at clearing free radicals.

Of course, raw eggs shouldn't be consumed by young children and pregnant women. But they shouldn't really be on the sauce in the first place. Which brings me to the world's only foolproof hangover cure.

Don't get drunk in the first place.

Chilli Sauce Score: ♪♪

IT'S A MAD, MAD, MAD, MAD WORLD

(1963, Dir. Stanley Kramer)

The bit where Ethel Merman slips on a banana skin

 When it comes to all-star casts, this mad-cap chase in pursuit of a stolen $350,000 certainly outshines most. Spencer Tracy, Milton Berle, Sid Caesar, Mickey Rooney, Phil Silvers, Jimmy Durante, Terry-Thomas, Peter Falk, Jack Benny, Buster Keaton, Jerry Lewis, the Three Stooges... and actress/song-belter Ethel Merman slipping on a banana skin in the final scene. The banana skin is a comic chestnut, so to speak. But is it really as slippery as the evidence of all those unfortunates we've seen sliding across the silver screen would suggest?

It's not just the cinema which portrays the banana as more slippery than an eel on a sledge. Even the hi-tech world of computer games has been known to use this ultimately low-tech yellow peril, with both Nintendo's *Donkey Kong* and *Mario Kart* employing a deviously placed banana skin to send players hurtling out of the game. Neither are banana-related accidents confined to computer or silver screens. In 2001, over 300 incidents were recorded in the UK. Most were caused by slipping on a skin. The rest were caused by... well, you can use your imagination. The situation was worse in early 20th-century America. Increased shipping and onboard refrigeration had made bananas the most popular fruit in the country. However there were few, if any, litter laws so skins were discarded as soon as they were finished with. The problem became so bad that urban street sanitation systems were actually developed specifically to deal with them.

But just how slippery are the skins? Researchers at the University of Sheffield thought they'd find out by using a machine called a pendulum tester. This is the standard device used by the UK Health and Safety Laboratory to measure what is known as pedestrian slip resistance; basically, it measures how slippery a surface is for pedestrians to walk on. The machine consists of a pendulum arm on which a section of rubber has been placed to replicate the sole of a pedestrian's shoe. The pendulum swings down and strikes whatever floor surface is being tested and the friction – or lack of it – is recorded.

For the banana test, skins were placed on a granite surface with the yellow side then the white side upwards, with both new and old skins. It perhaps didn't take a machine to tell the researchers that it doesn't matter which way up the skin is. The white inside is more slippery but when this was facing upwards the slippage occurred between the skin and the rubber, while if it was facing downwards the white part slipped more against the floor. What did make a difference was whether the banana skin was fresh or old. The former hardly lowered the friction between 'shoe' and floor at all. But with old, brown and soggy skins, the friction was dramatically reduced to seriously slippery levels. So it turns out that bananas can cause people to do their best Torvill and Dean impression. But ideally they should be old and brown (the fruit not the people) whereas the 'stunt' bananas in the movies are definitely young and yellow.

But then, Hollywood has always favoured youth and beauty over age.

Chilli Sauce Score: 🌶

CARRY ON ABROAD

(1972, Dir. Gerald Thomas)

The bit where an aphrodisiac drink makes people see others in their underwear

 Wundatours package holiday rep Kenneth Williams takes a group of English holidaymakers to the Spanish resort of Elsbels. Actually the whole film was shot in and around Pinewood studios, with the studio car park covered in sand. But that doesn't stop a whole host of package holiday clichés from being wheeled out, from a half-finished hotel and inclement weather to a good deal of hanky-panky, greatly assisted by the local tipple "Liquera por l'amoura", sneakily poured into a bowl of punch. Whatever's in the liquor, it sure has amazing qualities. On drinking it, the *Carry On* crew become even more lecherous than normal, to the extent that they start seeing each other in just their underwear. But could a drink really have such potently passionate effects?

Not according to the kill-joy US Food and Drug Administration who have declared that aphrodisiac foodstuffs and remedies have no effect on humans' sex drive. However they also admitted that their findings "clash with a 5,000-year tradition of pursuing sexual betterment through use of plants, drugs and magic". 5,000 years is long time to be hoodwinked by history's love potion-flogging Del Boys. Surely something must work?

For instance, oysters have been a considered an aphrodisiac since the time of Ancient Greece ("aphrodisiacs" are named after Aphrodite, the Greek goddess of love, beauty and sexuality). And there may be some truth to the legend, since oysters contain high quantities of zinc, which stimulates blood flow. In Asia, ginger has long been believed to increase passion, and it can indeed make the tongue tingle and lips swell. Similarly, spicy ingredients such as chilli are often put forward, as their "heat" can increase the heart rate. However, Asia is also known for some rather less palatable love potions, ranging from bat blood and rhino horn to shark fins and reindeer penises. (Watch out, Rudolph!) Men in ancient India were wont to sip on milk flavoured with goat testicles, which requires a lot more balls than the honeyed mead that mediaeval Englishmen were lucky enough to believe would do the trick.

One of the most notorious aphrodisiacs is Spanish fly, which is actually the remains of dried beetles. When alive, these beetles secrete an acid-like juice when threatened. When ground up and ingested, the beetle and its juice pass through the body before entering the urogenital tract. This leads to an itching and swelling of the genitals which was once assumed to be sexual arousal. Now it is known that Spanish fly can also cause kidney damage, convulsions and even death. It might be better to stick to coffee then – at least if you're of advanced years. A study of nearly 2,000 over-60s by the University of Michigan found that those who drank at least one cup of coffee a day engaged in more sexual activity than those who didn't. However, the suspicion is that this might simply be because they were awake more. In fact, there is no hard and fast evidence that any food or drink, or any ingredient therein, is an aphrodisiac – at least not with the potency to make someone make a pass at the nearest passerby.

But what if, as in the film, the drink you'd just had made you hallucinate? What if it was absinthe? Banned in many places today, this infamous liquor was most popular amongst creative types in 19th-century Europe and, in particular, France. The drink's name comes from the ingredient *Artemisia absinthium*, known as wormwood. This plant contains the neurotoxin thujone, which is chemically similar to THC, the active ingredient in marijuana. The accepted way of taking a glass of absinthe is to hold a sugar lump in a slotted spoon over your glass and then to pour water through the spoon so that it mixes with and sweetens the

absinthe, turning it from a transparent green to an opaque off-white. Artists and writers were particularly drawn to the drink because it was supposed to free the imagination. Oscar Wilde wrote, "After the first glass you see things as you wish they were. After the second, you see things as they are not. Finally you see things as they really are, and that is the most horrible thing in the world." But the reality is that you'd have to drink absinthe in silly quantities to take in enough thujone for it to start bending your mind. All the evidence suggest it's the alcohol in the drink that makes people see things like pink elephants parading across the ceiling.

Or the cast of a long-running British comedy series parading around in their underwear.

Chilli Sauce Score: ♪♪♪♪

CASINO ROYALE

(2006, Dir. Martin Campbell)

The bit where Daniel Craig doesn't care whether his martini is shaken or stirred

 Forget saving us all from the evil schemes of psychotic supervillains, wooing some of the world's most beautiful women, jumping out of planes without a parachute, or driving tanks, moon buggies and DB5s. Surely James Bond's most extraordinary talent is his ability to handle numerous vodka martinis, a cocktail that mixes its alcohol… with yet more alcohol. Bond reboot *Casino Royale* refreshes many of the film series' most recognisable features – and even has Bond not giving a fig how his martini is prepared. But what is the correct way to make this classic tipple?

The martini is thought to have been invented in 1862 at the Occidental Hotel, San Francisco, where guests would drink it before taking the evening ferry to the town of Martinez across the bay. The original cocktail consisted of two ounces of Italian sweet vermouth, one ounce of sweet gin, two dashes of maraschino cherry liquid and one dash of bitters, and was served with a twist of lemon. Over the years, the martini's ingredients were simplified and the drink became drier, with less vermouth added.

Indeed, the quest to prepare the driest martini seems to have been something of an obsession for certain drinkers. Noël Coward recommended "filling a glass with gin and then waving it in the general direction of Italy" whilst Alfred Hitchcock preferred five parts gin and a quick glance at a bottle of vermouth. Ernest Hemingway, a man's man's man, liked to order a "Montgomery", which was a martini of fifteen parts gin to one part vermouth: the same as the odds in his favour that Field Marshal Montgomery wanted to see before going into battle.

The first mention of vodka being used in a martini was in the 1950s, and it was in that decade that the James Bond novels popularized the vodka martini. However, in the first book, *Casino Royale* (1953), Bond drinks a vesper martini of three parts Gordon's gin, one part Russian vodka and a half measure of Kina Lillet aperitif, shaken until ice-cold and served with a slice of lemon. Indeed Daniel Craig describes the making of a vesper in great detail during the film *Casino Royale*. But it's after his defeat at poker by Le Chiffre that he returns to his favourite, the vodka martini.

But should it be shaken or stirred? According to the present-day bartenders at London's Dukes Hotel which, legend has it, provided Ian Fleming with the inspiration for the "shaken, not stirred" line, the answer is in fact neither. Their vodka martini (which should technically be called a Bradford to distinguish it from a gin martini) is made by putting three drops of extra dry vermouth in a chilled martini glass, followed by Polish vodka that has been frozen for 24 hours. Next, oil from the peel of an organic, Sicilian lemon is added, before the peel is rubbed around the edge of the glass and then dropped into the cocktail. No ice, no shaking, no stirring.

Indeed, shaking a gin-based martini is believed to "bruise" the alcohol, resulting in a somewhat bitter taste. Bond's martinis, however, are made with vodka and, crucially, vodka prior to the 1960s (at the time the first novels were written) was predominately refined from potatoes. Using potatoes rather than grain makes the vodka slightly oily. So Bond is right to ask bartenders to give his martinis a good shake, as this helps to disperse the oil. Incidentally, real shaken martinis appear cloudy in the glass, unlike the cocktails mixed in the films.

There may be one further reason why 007 likes his martinis served just so. According to a study conducted at the University of Western Ontario in Canada, the shaking of a martini helps to break down the hydrogen peroxide it contains, thus improving

its antioxidant capacity, which in turn reduces the risk of heart disease. Perhaps this is one of the reasons – or so the study suggests – why Bond is as fit as a fiddle.

But I reckon they've had too many Montgomerys.

Chilli Sauce Score: ♪♪

LARRY CROWNE

(2011, Dir. Tom Hanks)

The bit where a margarita gives Julia Roberts brain-freeze

Directed by Tom Hanks, starring Tom Hanks, co-produced by Tom Hanks, co-written by Tom Hanks... it's no surprise that *Larry Crowne* is a thoroughly *nice* film. Hanks plays the ever-optimistic Larry, who is made redundant from his long-term job and decides to enrol in a community college where he meets a group of loveable oddballs who like to ride around on mopeds. At college, Larry falls for a teacher called Mercedes, played by Julia Roberts, who with her cynicism and disillusionment at her profession gives the film some well-needed oomph. Mercedes is also partial to a drink or two, and makes a blender-full of frozen margaritas which end up giving her the type of headache known as brain-freeze. But why should ingesting something cold give you brain-freeze, and what can be done to get rid of it?

Mercedes' taste in cocktails is shared by many: the margarita is one of the most popular around the world: the United States even holds a National Margarita Day on 22 February each year. It's made by mixing tequila, an orange-flavoured liqueur such as triple sec, and lime (or, occasionally, lemon) juice. It can be served straight up, on the rocks or (as in the film) blended with ice, and often comes with salt on the glass rim. Yet despite its popularity, no one really knows who invented the margarita.

One of the best-known stories involves Dallas socialite, Margaret "Margarita" Sames. She was renowned in the 1940s for throwing extravagant parties at her holiday home in Acapulco, and credits herself with inventing the drink at one such party in 1948. The problem with this story is that tequila brand José Cuervo were running margarita-themed advertisements in 1945.

177

Another story asserts that a restaurant-owner in Tijuana, Mexico, called Carlos "Danny" Herrera invented the drink in 1938 for a showgirl called Marjorie King. Why the cocktail wasn't therefore named "the Marjorie" is lost in the mists of time. A third version involves one Danny "No Nickname" Negrete who, in 1936, supposedly created the cocktail at the Garci Crespo Hotel in Mexico as a wedding present for his sister-in-law, Margarita.

So what about brain-freeze? Perhaps we should call it by its scientific name, *sphenopalatine ganglioneuralgia*. On the other hand, perhaps not, as it isn't easy to say after a couple of cocktails. Why can eating cold food cause such a shocking headache? In fact, only about one-third of people suffer from brain-freeze. But that doesn't make it any less painful for those who do, and the phenomenon has even been the subject of scientific papers, such as *Ice cream evoked headaches (ICE-H) study: randomised trial of accelerated versus cautious ice cream eating regimen* by Maya and Janusz Kaczorowski. "Accelerated ice cream eating": now that sounds like a fun study.

When a large quantity of cold food or liquid in is taken into the mouth, some of it inevitably touches the hard palate in the roof of the mouth. Behind this palate is a bunch of nerves which acts as a thermostat for the brain. The main nerve, called the sphenopalatine nerve, is very sensitive to changes in temperature, and when ice cream or the like is shovelled into the mouth it sends signals to the brain to the effect that the next ice age has suddenly arrived. In response, the blood vessels surrounding the brain shrink. But when the brain realises that the sphenopalatine nerve has somewhat overreacted, warm blood rushes back into the blood vessels, and this is what causes the migraine-like pain. And it's also why there's often a delay between putting something cold in your mouth and when brain-freeze hits.

So how to get rid of it? Sipping a warm drink can stop the nerves behind the hard palate from overreacting, similarly putting your tongue against the roof of your mouth or even pressing your

thumb against your palate. But, sadly, the easiest thing to do is to avoid putting so much ice cream, sorbet, frappuchino or frozen margarita into your mouth in the first place.

As they say, there's no pleasure without pain.

Chilli Sauce Score: ♪

EAST OF EDEN

(1955, Dir. Elia Kazan)

The bit where Mastodon flesh is still tasty after thousands of years

 This was the only film starring James Dean to be released during his lifetime. Yet everything that made him one of the United States' great cultural icons is here: the young man ridden with angst and desperate for approval, but whose emotional honesty merely serves to highlight the brutal gap between one generation and the next. Dean plays Cal Trask, whose father (Raymond Massey) is trying to develop a way to keep vegetables fresh while they're being transported over long distances. Trask Sr experiments with blocks of ice to keep lettuces fresh, mentioning that a mastodon had been dug up in Siberia after being buried in ice for thousands of years, and that its meat was still as "sweet as a pork chop". But doesn't the idea of a prehistoric animal's flesh still being edible actually smell quite fishy?

What exactly was a mastodon? Its genus name *Mammut* gives a clue because, although mastodons were different in several respects to mammoths, they were indeed a type of prehistoric elephant. Mastodons evolved much earlier than mammoths (about 20 million years ago compared to two million years ago for mammoths) and were slightly smaller (a mere 4 metres long and two tons in weight) with flatter heads. They also fed on the leaves of trees and plants, whereas mammoths tended to graze on grass. However, Mr Trask gets it wrong when he says that the mastodon dug up in Siberia had been buried for thousands of years. In fact, the European mastodon died out millions of years ago. It was the North American mastodon that survived much longer, persisting into the last Ice Age (around 10,000 B.C.).

But let's not split hairs – or hairy mammoths. Ignoring the fact that a mastodon from Siberia would have been buried much longer than is reckoned in the film, could the ice it had been buried under have kept its flesh edible? Numerous mastodon and mammoth carcasses have been excavated around the world, ranging from a few bones to specimens with skin, hair and internal organs all preserved. And it is indeed in the heart-stopping chill of Siberia that some of the best-preserved remains have been found.

There are many travellers' tales of adventurous types (usually on the point of starvation) stumbling upon frozen carcasses, defrosting them over campfires and tucking into hearty meals of roasted prehistoric elephant flesh. In 1872, *The New York Times* published an account of French adventurers in Russia who claimed to have found so many well-preserved mammoth specimens that they "lived entirely on mammoth meat, broiled, roasted and baked". In 1912, novelist James Oliver Curwood told the *Chicago Tribune* of the time he had dined on mastodon with some local Canadian natives. Curwood described the meat as "deep red or mahogany". He also said that it tasted "old and dry". Could this have been down to an incompetent cook rather than the meat itself? Unfortunately not. Curwood's disappointing experience seems to have been shared by a Russian zoologist, Alexei Tikhonov, who once tried a bite of mammoth flesh (which we may presume tastes similar to mastodon) and said that "it was awful. It tasted like meat left too long in the freezer" – which of course is basically what it was. And it appears that he got off lightly. A 1961 article in the magazine *Science* stated that, of 39 carcasses that had been uncovered, only four were reasonably complete and of these "all the frozen specimens were rotten."

Sweet as a pork chop? No, James Dean's dad was telling porkies.

Chilli Sauce Score: ♪♪♪♪

BEN-HUR

(1959, Dir. William Wyler)

The bit where Charlton Heston is encouraged to burp after eating

Forget the 11 Academy Awards; the 15,000 extras; the 1,000,000 props; the epic story of Prince Judah Ben-Hur, who is betrayed and sold into slavery before gaining his revenge and witnessing Christ's crucifixion. Forget even the fast, furious, totally realistic and blessedly CGI-free chariot race. Instead, consider the scene when Charlton Heston is dining with an Arab sheikh and, at the behest of a wise old man called Balthazar, burps to show his gratitude. Is this good manners or bad?

The main cause of burping, which is also known as eructation, is eating or drinking too fast. This causes air to be swallowed (termed "aerophagia") and later expelled. Drinking anything fizzy – from champagne downwards – can also cause burping, though in this case it's carbon dioxide rather than air that's expelled. On average we burp about fifteen times a day. The delightful sound of a burp is caused by the vibration of the oesophageal sphincter as gas passes through it. The current world record for the loudest burp is 109.9 decibels, set by Paul Hunn from London. This is considerably louder than an electric drill and not far off the volume of a clap of thunder. Well done, Paul. Your mother must be really proud.

In the western world, eructation at the dinner table is largely frowned upon, though we have plenty of other strange customs to remember at dinner time. In Austria and Germany, for example, it's a must to look someone in the eye when you clink glasses with them. Also in Germany, it's seen as bad manners to cut your potatoes with a knife: crushing them with a fork is the way to do it. In France, chefs will come at you with a cleaver if you

add condiments to your food before you've tasted it. And it's *de rigueur* to have both hands visible at all times to show that no hanky panky is going on below the table.

Moving eastward, when you find yourself eating a whole fish in Poland you mustn't turn it over to get to the flesh on the other side… because you'll also be turning over the fisherman's boat. You must also be careful if you decide to give a toast when dining in Hungary. Mispronounce the most common Hungarian toast *Egészségedre* and, instead of saying "To your health", you'll end up toasting "To your arse". Similarly, making a toast in Japan can be embarrassing if you decide to use the English phrase, "Chin chin" – which also happens to be colloquial Japanese for "penis".

Back to burping. Yes, eructation is considered impolite across most of the West. However, in Germany there are those who think the opposite and will quote the religious reformer Martin Luther who said, "Warum ruelpset und pfurzet ihr nicht, hat es euch nicht geschmecket?" This translates as, "Why burpest and fartest thou not, didn't you fancy the grub?" And the Germans' view is shared elsewhere. In some parts of Turkey, you honour the chef if you burp after eating. This is also true across parts of the Middle East (where *Ben-Hur* was set). And sometimes burping once isn't enough, with certain cultures believing that if a person doesn't burp at least three times after a meal, this signifies that they think they haven't been given enough food by their miserly host.

All of which proves that Heston's wind was no wind-up.

Chilli Sauce Score: 𝄢

BEASTS

"Alright, alright, Mickey's a
mouse, Donald's a duck,
Pluto's a dog. What's Goofy?"
Stand by Me

MONTY PYTHON AND THE HOLY GRAIL

(1975, Dir. Terry Gilliam and Terry Jones)

The bit where talk turns to coconut-carrying swallows

If ever there was an ideal film for this book, this is it. As soon as King Arthur (Graham Chapman) trots into shot, pretending to ride a horse, with his faithful servant Patsy (Terry Gilliam) providing clip-clop sound effects with two halves of a coconut shell, it's clear that the conventions of cinema are in for a sound thrashing. Indeed castle guards Michael Palin and John Cleese do much of our work themselves, with a methodical deconstruction of the logic behind King Arthur's assertion that a swallow could have carried Patsy's coconut from the tropics to England. However, is their argument correct as well as comical?

The original script for the film called for the characters to ride real horses. Happily the budget was too small, so it was decided that the Pythons would pretend to ride horses while their servants banged coconut shells together. And in another type of nutshell, here is the castle guards' argument for why a swallow could not carry a coconut:

- A 5-ounce bird could not carry a 1-pound coconut.
- In order to maintain air-speed velocity, a swallow needs to beat its wings 43 times every second.
- It *could* be carried by an African, as opposed to a European swallow.
- But African swallows are not migratory.

They're right. A swallow weighing five ounces (142 g) could not possibly carry a coconut weighing one pound (454 g). In reality

no swallow weighs even as much as five ounces. A 54-year survey of 26,285 European swallows *(Hirundo rustica)* by the Avian Demography Unit of the University of Cape Town found that the average adult European swallow had a wing length of 12.2 cm and a body mass of 20.3 grams, that is, about 0.7 ounces. In terms of air-speed velocity, a swallow would need to have swallowed a good deal of Red Bull to be able to beat its wings 43 times every second. A study of two European swallows flying in a Swedish wind tunnel showed that they flew at only 7–9 beats per second, giving them a maximum unladen airspeed velocity of 39 km/h.

But what about an African swallow? Well, there are 47 different species of swallow in Africa, yet none is called the African swallow. The names of two species are close: the West African swallow *(Hirundo domicella)* and the South African swallow *(Hirundo spilodera)*. Although not completely non-migratory, as suggested in the film, neither gets as far as the shores of England. And neither is anywhere near big enough to carry a coconut.

So when King Arthur asserts that a swallow could carry a coconut, we should really give him the bird.

Chilli Sauce Score: 〟〟〟〟〟

SEVEN SAMURAI

(1954, Dir. Akira Kurosawa)

The bit where a samurai catches a fish with his hands

If you've watched *The Magnificent Seven*, *The Dirty Dozen* or *Ocean's Eleven* then you will have seen three of the many films which owe their existence to Japan's most celebrated cinematic offering. This is the film that started one of the most popular storylines of twentieth-century cinema, where a band of differing but heroic characters comes together to accomplish a specific mission.

Six fully-fledged and one would-be samurai are hired to protect a mountain village from bandits. The villagers have no money but can offer food as payment. Gisaku the village elder has suggested they "find hungry samurai", and it's the comic character Kikuchiyo, the would-be samurai, who shows just how starving he is by jumping into a river and catching a fish with his bare hands. But is such a feat possible, or have we fallen for it hook, line and sinker?

Atemmpting to grab a fish as it swims by is always going to be an unreliable way of staving off starvation. However, if you've found a stretch of river inhabited by trout then there is a way to catch them without using a rod, line or net: the way of the trout tickler. This is a skill with a long (if illicit) history: trout tickling is even mentioned in Shakespeare's *Twelfth Night*, when the despised Malvolio is described as "the trout that must be caught with tickling" (Act 2, Scene 5). With no equipment needed, it's long been a favourite technique of the poaching fraternity who found that it was easier to persuade gamekeepers of their honest intentions if they weren't carrying a twenty-foot fishing rod.

So how's it done? Trout tickling involves rubbing a trout's underbelly with your fingers. This encourages it to enter a trance-like state in which it can be plucked out of the water with the

189

greatest of ease. That's the theory. Actually doing it successfully is, if not quite a different kettle of fish, not without its problems. For one thing, merely approaching a river is likely to send a trout darting beneath the bank. So a softly, softly approach is required. If you see a trout disappear under the bank, lie down on your stomach and slowly approach the place where the fish was last seen. Then slide both hands very slowly into the water and gradually move them inwards towards the bank. This needs to be done little by little – trout tickling is about as much a spectator sport as watching paint dry.

Once you have located your trout, begin to rub its underbelly while also trying to identify which end is its head and which its tail. Then slowly move your hands towards its head before firmly gripping it around its gills. If all has gone to plan the trout should be completely relaxed, enabling you simply to stand up and move away from the river. Yet this can be difficult when you're lying on your front and have both hands full of wet fish. The important thing is to avoid throwing the trout onto the bank, since it's likely to jump straight back in.

Even if your trout-tickling technique is excellent, there's one more problem you face. It's illegal. Many parts of the country have at one time or another introduced specific bylaws forbidding the ancient practice of tickling. But the Salmon and Freshwater Fisheries Act 1975, and in particular Section 27, created a blanket ban across England and Wales. Section 27a made it an offence to fish or take fish with any unlicensed instrument or by using a licensed instrument in any way other than in accordance with the terms of the licence. As the rotters at the Environment Agency won't issue a licence for "hands", the game is up. Although this hasn't stopped a few people from trying – and being prosecuted.

So unless you're a samurai in the sixteenth century, if you try to catch a fish by hand you'll have had your chips.

Chilli Sauce Score:

THE PALEFACE

(1948, Dir. Norman Z. McLeod)

The bit where Bob Hope tells a horse that its wisdom teeth need to be removed

 Hope plays "Painless" Peter Potter, dentist and coward. Jane Russell is Calamity Jane, on a mission to discover who's selling guns to the Indians. As part of her cover, Jane marries Potter and they join a wagon train. Cue wisecracks from Hope – "Brave men run in my family" – an Academy Award for the song *Buttons and Bows*, and lots of general silliness, including a dental inspection of a horse. The verdict is that the animal's wisdom teeth need to be taken out. But do horses have wisdom teeth, and, more importantly for anyone who's averse to spending too much time at the dentist's, why do *we* have them?

Wisdom teeth form the third and last set of molar teeth and their original purpose was to help us grind down food. But as humankind acquired the habit of cooking, there came to be less need for Desperate Dan-style jaw muscles, and our mouths shrunk as a result. This is one possible reason why wisdom teeth can cause over-crowding in the mouth. The other possibility is that today's adults are better at keeping their teeth for longer than generations gone by. According to this explanation, the purpose of wisdom teeth is to act as back-ups in case other teeth break or fall out (similarly, sharks have extra rows of teeth). But because we're no longer gap- and black-toothed, our wisdom teeth have nothing to do apart from make dentists money.

But what about other animals? Many mammals have room for the equivalent of a third set of molars, as their jaws tend to be more commodious (perhaps because they haven't mastered the art of frying a fillet steak). And horses do have another sort of tooth that has a similar role to wisdom teeth – that is, it has no role. Confusingly, it's called a wolf tooth. Horses' wolf teeth come in different shapes, sizes and positions but are typically found in the space between the incisors and the molars. Around 50% of domestic horses have at least one wolf tooth, usually in the upper jaw. The teeth often appear as small pegs with sharp points and can cause pain when they push against their owner's other teeth. They may also cause problems if the horse is wearing a bit. Some two- or three-year-old horses shed their wolf teeth, whereas others have them removed by an equine dental specialist.

So humans aren't the only ones for whom useless gnashers can be a real pain. And you heard that straight from the horse's mouth.

Chilli Sauce Score: *)*

ON THE WATERFRONT

(1954, Dir. Elia Kazan)

The bit where pigeons mate for life

With Academy Awards for Best Picture, Best Actor and Best Director (amongst five others), this tale of mob corruption on the docks also made it into the Vatican's list of the greatest films of all time, narrowly pipping Paris Hilton in *The Hottie and the Nottie*. Method-acting Marlon Brando is ex-boxing ("I coulda been a contender") dockworker Terry Malloy, who also happens to know quite a bit about pigeons. But do the birds really mate for life, as he claims?

Pigeons are descended from domesticated rock doves. Feral pigeons live from three to five years and are found throughout Europe and in Africa, North America, South America and Asia. As anyone will know who has dropped a greasy chip and seen it swooped upon within seconds, pigeons are not picky when it comes to what they eat (though who bought the greasy chips in the first place?). This is probably due to the fact that they have only 40 taste buds compared to our 10,000. Compared to feral pigeons, captive pigeons – which tend to have a more wholesome diet – are veritable Methuselahs: they can live up to thirty-five years.

Both wild and tame pigeons are skilled in the art of romance. When a male pigeon begins to court a female he will follow her around while bowing his head, fanning his tail and making affectionate cooing noises. If this works, the pair move on to the pigeon equivalent of a snog on the dancefloor, with the female holding the male's beak in her own while they shuffle around. Things move forward pretty fast now, ending up with the male on his partner's back for a short bout of mating. If all goes well, the female will then lay two eggs in a nest she has built from material collected by the male. And so the couple settle down to a life of wedded bliss together.

Or not, as the case may be. Although in the past it was believed that over 92% of bird species were monogamous, it seems that many are partial to a bit on the side. That isn't to say they don't give the impression of being devoted to each other until death do them part. But science has shown that when it comes to sex, almost anything goes. Indeed DNA tests have revealed that between 10% and 40% of the offspring of birds which were thought to be monogamous were actually fathered by another male. And perhaps most shocking of all, 25% of migrating females were shown to be carrying sperm even before they arrived at their breeding grounds.

Scandalous!

Maybe it's not so surprising then that in 2010 in Gloucestershire an event was witnessed which until that point had been considered one of the rarest in nature: a swan divorce. It happened when male swan Sarindi turned up after his annual migration from artic Russia, not with his usual mate Saruni, but with a new bird called Sarind. Shortly afterwards, Saruni turned up with her new man, a swan named Surune. One bird expert suggested that the divorce was caused by a failure to breed.

But it seems that too much bedroom activity might have been the real cause of the split.

Chilli Sauce Score: ♪ ♪ ♪ ♪

THE HANGOVER
PART II

(2011, Dir. Todd Phillips)

The bit where a monkey enjoys a cigarette

"It happened again," says Bradley Cooper. And it certainly has. Taking the same premise as the first film – a group of friends wake up after a bachelor party with no idea where they are or what happened the night before – *Part II* transfers the mayhem from Las Vegas to Bangkok. It's not quite as consistently funny as its predecessor, but still manages to pack in more than its fair share of shock and awe, from severed fingers and unwanted face tattoos to kidnapping a monk and intimate relations with a ladyboy. One of the stars of the film is Crystal, a capuchin monkey, who plays a drug-dealing primate with a smoking habit. But can animals become addicted to cigarettes?

Crystal looked a million dollars on the red carpet at the film's premiere, wearing a pink gown and pearls. But she's used to the limelight, with twenty films under her belt, including *George of the Jungle*, *American Pie* and *Night at the Museum*. With such extensive acting experience, it's no surprise that she puts in a great performance in *The Hangover Part II*. But did she really smoke? Director Todd Phillips was originally quoted as saying that Crystal became addicted to smoking during filming. And the film doesn't carry the usual "No animals were harmed in the making of this film" disclaimer issued by the American Humane Association. Phillips later confessed that he had been joking and Crystal's trainer confirmed that the cigarettes were ceramic and that the smoke was added in post-production. But that doesn't stop other animals being addicted to the demon weed.

The most famous example is probably Charlie the South

195

African chimp. Charlie acquired his habit when visitors to his zoo in Bloemfontein started throwing him lit cigarettes. For years his keepers tried to get Charlie to kick the habit, but to no avail. And when thousands of people began to flock the zoo just to see Charlie puffing away, the zoo's owners realised they had a cash cow (or chimp) on their hands. Sadly, Charlie passed away in 2010 at the age of 52. The cause of death? Natural causes. Indeed, Charlie had lived for ten years longer than your average, non-smoking chimpanzee.

From the most famous example to what must be one of the weirdest: Po the pit viper (or the Taiwanese beauty snake, depending who you believe). Here's another case of a discarded cigarette kick-starting the creature's habit. Owner Sho Lau says, "He is very tame and one day when I threw a cigarette butt away he went for it and seemed to enjoy having it in his mouth." Now Po enjoys nothing more than a quick puff first thing in the morning and last thing at night.

And from the weirdest to perhaps the most distressing example – smoking beagles. Between 1967 and 1970, the American Cancer Society funded a Dr Oscar Auerbach in his experiments to "effectively refute contentions by cigarette-manufacturing interests that there was no cigarette-cancer link". Dr Auerbach's first experiment involved twenty beagles who had been subjected to "debarking", where tissue was removed from their vocal cords to keep them quiet in the laboratory. The dogs were then given tracheotomies, after which tubes were inserted into their necks, with filterless lit cigarettes inserted into the other end of the tubes. The beagles were forced to smoke up to 12 cigarettes a day for a whole year, which Dr Auerbach equated to two packs a day for humans. Some of the dogs became addicted to nicotine, wagging their tails when they knew the next cigarette was coming. And some did indeed develop cancer. Not that the tobacco industry – or their customers – paid the slightest bit of notice.

As it turns out, smoking isn't the only animal addiction.

Myrmecomany (from the ancient Greek *myrmex* meaning ant and *mania*) is a behaviour seen in certain bird species such as ravens, blackbirds and parrots. The bird sits on an ants' nest and allows the ants to crawl all over it before performing a series of strange contortions. Some scientists believe that the birds use the formic acid that is secreted by the ants to clean their plumage. But others think that the birds are addicted to the tingling feeling that the acid produces. Other avian junkies include Australian red-brown finches, which have been observed landing on smoking tree trunks after bush fires. The finches breathe in the smoke which makes them extend their feathers before falling from the tree in a state of intoxication. They then repeat the ritual. Other birds are reported to get their kicks from "substances" as varied as caterpillars, mothballs and ashes.

It's not just birds. About 50% of cats have an overwhelming attraction to the plant *Nepeta cataria*, known as catnip, which they sniff and eat to give them pleasure. Whereas booze is the poison for green vervet monkeys on the island of St Kitts, where they like to take their alcohol in the form of fermenting sugar cane. Tests on the monkeys have shown that they each fall into one of four categories: binge drinker, steady drinker, social drinker and teetotaller. And a similar situation exists in parts of Africa, where the marula tree grows. The tree's fruit ripens and ferments very easily, and animal who eat it rapidly become intoxicated. Occasions have been witnessed when every animal near a marula tree, from monkeys to elephants, has been drunk as a lord.

And that's what you call a wild party.

Chilli Sauce Score: ♪♪

STAND BY ME

(1986, Dir. Rob Reiner)

The bit where the boys brush leeches off their bodies

A simple story (based on the novella *The Body* by Stephen King) but a great film. Set in Oregon in the summer of 1959, it's a coming-of-age adventure about a group of friends on an expedition to find the body of a missing boy. Full of great performances and tall stories – who can forget the blueberry-pie-eating chunderfest? – the film also includes a scene where they end up covered in leeches. The boys are predictably grossed out, especially as one of the little suckers has found a nice warm home down one of the lads' underpants. But all's well that ends well, and the leeches come off easily. But was removing them too easy?

Leeches are common in many parts of the world; some are aquatic whilst others live in vegetation. They sense their prey – warm-blooded animals – through odour and vibrations. And when they've got stuck in, they can gorge themselves on blood until they've gained up to ten times their weight, with a single feeding giving them enough sustenance for several months. They have three jaws each holding up to 120 teeth. And with thirty-two brains each, they're probably dead clever too.

Covering up and using repellent are the best ways to avoid getting bitten by a leech, but they do have a habit of worming (should that be leeching?) their way onto the bodies of even the most protected travellers. When they do, they release an anaesthetic which means you won't even know you're being attacked. What's more, leeches deploy an anticoagulant to keep your blood flowing as they tuck in: leech bites can bleed for ten hour. However, it's not all bad. Leeches don't cause massive blood loss and they don't carry diseases. Indeed they have been used by physicians since 1000 B.C. because it used to be believed that

their blood-letting abilities could prevent and cure a wide range of conditions. In 1830 alone, London hospitals used a staggering 7 million leeches.

But how easy is it to get rid of one? Well, one way is to bide your time, because leeches simply drop off when they've taken enough blood. If you'd prefer not to wait, it isn't quite as simple as brushing the little critter off. Instead you need to find the oral sucker at the small end of the leech. Then you put your finger on your skin next to the sucker and, using your fingernail, carefully push the sucker away from the wound. Now you need to move fast. The leech will still be clinging onto you by a sucker at its rear end. You need to dislodge this before it re-attaches its mouth. A quick flick should suffice.

Speed is also of the essence in the not-very-nice-at-all event of a leech getting into your nose, mouth or ear, since it will expand and make extraction extremely difficult. In this instance, the application of strong alcohol can make the leech drop off. Otherwise the only thing is to puncture it with a sharp object. Whatever happens, don't try burning a leech off with a cigarette, applying salt or yanking the animal off. This tends to result in the leech regurgitating into the wound and causing infection.

So to those who think that leeches can simply be brushed off, there's only one thing to say. Suckers!

Chilli Sauce Score:)))）

LAW ABIDING CITIZEN

(2009, Dir. F. Gary Gray)

The bit where pufferfish poison leaves a murderer paralysed but pain-sensitive

 Gerard Butler plays the oddly-accented Clyde Sheldon (perhaps he studied at fellow-Scot Sean Connery's School of Interesting Inflections): a man who turns out to be anything but law-abiding. His thirst for vengeance is at least understandable, seeing as he witnessed the murder of both his wife and daughter. Its scope, which seems to encompass virtually everyone in the United States, is less so. And his methods, including being able to pop in and out of a prison's solitary confinement block at will, are even less so still. But does the film's general nonsense extend to using the liver of a pufferfish to paralyse one of the murderers before torturing him to death?

Clyde seems to have picked his poison carefully. He says that he chose the liver of the pufferfish because it contains a neurotoxin that will paralyse a person but leave them fully conscious and able to feel pain – and what he does to the man who murdered his family sure involves a lot of that. And yes, pufferfish (also known as balloon fish, blowfish, bubble fish, globefish, swellfish, toadfish, toadies, honey toads, and sea squab) are one of the deadliest of deadly creatures. In fact they're believed to be the second-most poisonous vertebrate after the Golden Poison Frog, with each fish containing large amounts of tetrodotoxin in its organs, especially the liver, ovaries and skin.

A neurotoxin that is hundreds of times deadlier than cyanide and has no known antidote, tetrodotoxin is a sodium channel blocker that prevents affected nerve channels from firing. And it can indeed paralyse a victim's muscles whilst leaving them fully conscious. However Clyde doesn't mention tetrodoxin's other symptoms, which range from tingling in the mouth, vomiting, diarrhoea, hypersalivation and hypotension, to low body temperature, a rapid, weak pulse, respiratory distress and, often, death.

The pufferfish's extreme toxicity means that the average person isn't likely to want to touch one with a bargepole. But hey, when have our friends in Japan ever been happy with average? So they only go and eat the little fishy devils. Raw. Yes, pufferfish is considered a delicacy in Japan, amongst (a very few) other nations. The Japanese name for the fish, and the dish made from it, is "fugu". The restaurant preparation of fugu is strictly controlled by law, with chefs having to undergo rigorous training to ensure that the toxic parts are removed and have not contaminated the rest of the fish. Some consider the liver (known as fugu kimo) the tastiest part, but it's also the most poisonous. In 1975, the late actor Bando Mitsugoro VIII ordered four fugu kimo in a restaurant. You'll notice I referred to him as 'the late'. He claimed he could withstand the poison; he couldn't. In 1984, Japan banned restaurants from serving fugu liver.

Wherever he is, Mitsugoro can console himself knowing that he is on a long and occasionally distinguished list of fugu victims, beginning with the crew of Captain Cook's Bounty. The ship's log for 7 September 1774 records that the crew ate some puffers that they had fished out of the Pacific before feeding the guts and bones to the pigs kept on board. Shortly afterwards, the crew experienced numbness and shortness of breath. The next morning the pigs were dead, presumably because they'd been fed the fishes' livers.

So in terms of the effects of pufferfish and neurotoxins, *Law Abiding Citizen* gets a very respectable Chilli Sauce Score. If only the rest of the film were as believable.

Chilli Sauce Score:)

CARRY ON CAMPING

(1969, Dir. Gerald Thomas)

The bit where the colour red attracts a bull

Nudge nudge, wink wink. It's the very British comedy film series again, full of busty girls, lecherous men and dodgy *double entendres*. Filmed in '69 (ooh-er missus), *Carry on Camping* is typical fare. We have a Sid Boggle, Farmer Fiddler, Dr Soaper and Miss Haggard. And we have Terry Scott playing a reluctant camper with the unusually sensible name of Peter Potter, who is persuaded by his braying wife that the best thing to do when confronted by a bull is to wave a red cloth at it. But do bulls that see red actually *see* red?

There are two kinds of photoreceptor situated in the retina at the back of the eye which, because of their shapes, are called rods and cones. Rods help us see in dim light but only show things in black and white, exactly as the world appears when we go outside at nightfall. Cones, on the other hand, only work in bright light but they give us the world in glorious technicolour. Humans have three types of cones, picking up either red, green or blue. It is by processing combinations of these primary colours that our brains are able to perceive all the other colours that we know.

However the sight of some people is colour-deficient because they lack one type of cone. And it's the same for bulls. The simple fact is that Terry Scott's cloth could have been green, orange or pink with yellow polka dots – because although bulls' eyes can perceive the colour blue, their photoreceptors can't distinguish between red and green. Bulls are red/green colour-blind and are more likely to react to a cloth not because it's red but because it's being waved around by a lunatic. The colour red has almost certainly become linked with furious ruminants because humans associate it with danger. It's the same but different with bullfighting. The bull is provoked by the matador's cape (called a muleta) because it's moving. But the probable reason why most capes are red is because it helps to hide the blood.

It may lack the power and presence of the mighty bull, but the humble mantis shrimp is the definite winner when it comes to colour perception. Like insects, these marine crustaceans possess compound eyes which are made up of thousands of rows of light-detectors called ommatidia. These are especially refined in the mantis shrimp, with a combination of photoreceptors and filters enabling it to perceive 100,000 colours, roughly ten times that of humans. But the real trick up a mantis shrimp's sleeve is its ability, unlike any other animal, to see circular polarized light. The photons in CPL travel in spirals, as opposed to linear polarized light where the photons travel in a regular up-and-down wavelength. The shrimps' eyes have special cells which can straighten out the photons in CPL, enabling them to perceive it. Mantis shrimps also have a patch of CPL-reflecting exoskeleten on their bodies, so it's likely that their visual ability has developed to help them communicate during territorial and sexual encounters.

So the mantis is definitely the colour king of the whole animal world. No bull.

Chilli Sauce Score: ♪ ♪ ♪ ♪

STARSKY AND HUTCH

(2004, Dir. Todd Phillips)

The bit where an iguana regrows its tail

An iguana-owning character called Huggy Bear played by a rapper named Snoop Dogg. This film could only ever go in the "Beasts" section of this book. Straight-laced and childlike David Starsky (Ben Stiller) shoots the tail off an iguana belonging to street-wise and super-cool Huggy Bear. But it's not the end of the world because, according to Mr Bear, the tail will grow back.

And the truth is, it might well do just that. However, most iguanas don't lose their tails because they've been shot by a trigger-happy undercover cop. They are more likely to divest themselves of their tails deliberately in an action called caudal autotomy (*caudum* in Latin means "tail" and *autotomy* is a combination of the Greek for "self" and "cut"). Other animals – including octopuses, crabs, lobsters, spiders and slugs – practice autotomy, ridding themselves of a body part when under attack. For iguanas, this usually happens when a predator manages to grab it by its tail. An iguana's tail contains muscle bundles which are attached to the tail's vertebrae and which the iguana can contract, breaking the vertebrae and thus the tail. Once it snaps off, the tail continues to wriggle around, drawing away the attention of the predator whilst the iguana legs it.

However because of the design of an iguana's tail, accidental tail loss does happen, especially in captivity. An iguana might hit its tail against its cage. A clumsy owner might inadvertently stand on it. Or a totally stupid owner might grab the iguana when it tries to run away. If your iguana does become parted from its tail, proper care is required to stem bleeding and prevent infection. And then it's a case of waiting and seeing. Because not all iguanas will grow

back their tails. If you – like Huggy Bear – believe that they do, you're probably confusing iguanas with geckos, who can grow a brand spanking new appendage inside a month. In contrast, tail regrowth for iguanas depends on a number of factors, including age, health and how far up the tail the amputation occurred. Even if the tail does grow back, it won't look like the original. Re-grown tails are shorter and more club-like than their predecessors and, like scar tissue, they have a different texture and colour from the rest of the iguana's body.

So it's probably just as well that the stylish Mr Bear didn't realise that his pet was going to end up with a stubby, discoloured rear end. That really would have been a sorry tale.

Chilli Sauce Score: ♪♪

THE TREE OF LIFE

(2011 Dir. Terrence Malick)

The bit where dinosaurs are different colours

When *The Tree of Life* was shown at the Cannes Film Festival it was both applauded and booed. And when an Italian cinema showed the film and the first two reels were accidentally switched, no one in the audience actually realised and thought it was all down to Terrence Malick's "crazy editing style". This pretty much sums up this ambitious, visually magnificent and often indecipherable story of a Texas family in the 1950s, interwoven with depictions of the creation of the universe and the beginnings of life on Earth. During the latter, we see different species of dinosaur in a forest and on a riverbank. Each kind has its own skin colour and markings. But how can Malick, or anyone else, know what colour the dinosaurs really were?

The word *dinosaur* was coined in 1842 by English biologist Sir Richard Owen from the Greek for "fearfully great lizard" (and not "terrible lizard" as is often supposed). But maybe that should be "terribly-coloured lizard". Because no one knows for sure what colours dinosaurs were. In virtually all books, films (*The Tree of Life* included) and museums, their skin colour is shown as being variously green, grey, brown or occasionally a daring orange, sometimes with markings but mostly without. And this tends to be because dinosaur designers (now there's a job) take their inspiration from other large reptiles like crocodiles, or furless animals such as rhinos.

But it's all guesswork. In fact, forget skin colour for a moment: we actually have no incontrovertible evidence as to what dinosaurs looked like at all. Yes, educated guesses can be made as to shape and posture by looking at the bone structures and appearances

of some present-day animals. But dinosaur skeletons are rarely found intact and for some species all there is to go on is a single, incomplete pile of bones. And even when a fossilized skeleton is found intact, how palaeontologists determine the way the muscles fitted over the frame, and the soft tissues over the muscles, and the skin over the soft tissues, and the frills, lips, noses… Well, your guess is as good as mine is (nearly) as good as theirs. It's simply impossible to deduce with complete accuracy the appearance of some creatures from their skeletons – no matter how many bones you find. Take the elephant and its trunk, or the toucan and its crazy beak, for instance.

Sometimes the accepted view among palaeontologists of a species' appearance changes radically. In the majority of representations before the 1980s, the ceratopsian group of dinosaurs was shown with crooked legs and bellies close to the ground like crocodiles. Now they tend to be depicted with straight legs and a posture that's closer to that of rhinos. But perhaps the uncertainty over appearance is understandable, given that scientists can't even agree whether dinosaurs were cold-blooded or warm-blooded – in which case they weren't lizards (terrible, fearfully great or otherwise) at all. Similarly, no one knows what dinosaurs' eyes looked like, whether their pupils were slits like reptiles', or round like birds'. So guess what? Dinosaurs that were believed to be mean, aggressive predators are generally depicted with evil-looking slits, whereas their poor, defenceless prey are given the dinosaur equivalent of round puppy-dog eyes.

Our lack of knowledge about their eyes is another reason why the "guesstimation" of dinosaurs' skin colour is so difficult. Often a certain colouration is chosen because it's assumed that the particular dinosaur species would have used camouflage as part of its defence strategy, so it's given a similar colour to its environment: green for jungles, yellow for deserts, and so on. But no one knows which colours dinosaur eyes could perceive. Camouflage may have been completely irrelevant.

However, all is not entirely lost when it comes to dinosaur colour. Recent discoveries by a team of Chinese and British scientists have uncovered the first real indications that at least some dinosaurs were brightly coloured. The discoveries were made in northeastern China and comprised the 125 million-year-old fossils of small meat-eating dinosaurs called theropods. These dinosaurs, from which birds are descended, were covered with primitive "protofeathers". Some of these feathers were found in the fossils and within them the scientists identified melanosomes. These microscopic structures form part of the pigment cells that give modern birds their colour. And the scientists were even able to tell which colours the dinosaur melanosomes produced. The dinosaur called Sinosauropteryx has been shown to have had an orange-coloured crest and black-grey stripes along its tail.

So we're just starting to gain some idea of dinosaur colouration. But it's really only the bare bones.

Chilli Sauce Score: ♪ ♪ ♪

GLADIATOR

(2000, Dir. Ridley Scott)

The bit where maggots help to clean a wound

Russell Crowe is Maximus Decimus Meridius, previously General of the Roman Army, now a gladiator grieving his murdered wife and son and intent on having his revenge in this life or the next. It's an Academy Award-winning and truly epic film, one that both relaunched the sword-and-sandals genre and provided the last role for the legendary Oliver Reed, (who in typical hell-raising, show-stealing form died half way through the production). Escaping execution only to discover that his family has been slaughtered, Maximus is captured by slave traders heading towards North Africa. En route, he drifts in and out of consciousness as he recovers from exhaustion and a nasty sword wound to his arm. The wound becomes infected with maggots, but one of Maximus' travelling companions tells him not to worry because the maggots will help to clean the wound.

In fact, maggots have been used to get rid of necrotic flesh throughout history. Prehistoric Australian Aborigines are believed to have used maggots to treat the wounded, while records suggest that Mayan Indians wrapped injuries with cloths which had been soaked in animal blood and then dried in the sun: it wasn't long before the movement of maggots was observed beneath the dressing. During the Napoleonic wars, surgeons like Baron Dominique-Jean Larrey observed how soldiers benefited from maggots infesting their wounds. One can only imagine the difficulties he must have faced as he tried to convince some grizzled old soldier with half an arm hanging off that allowing maggots to swarm over his wound and feast on his flesh was somehow a good idea. Yet the practice continued, and over a century later soldiers stationed in Burma during World

War II witnessed how villagers placed maggots in wounds and covered them with mud and grass.

It wasn't until the development of antibiotics, and in particular the commercial availability of penicillin from 1944, that the use of maggots declined. But it's hard to keep the little larvae down and by 2002 Maggot Debridement Therapy (MDT), as their use had become known, was again being practised in over 2,000 health care centres around the world. Exactly how maggots assist wound-healing is now properly understood, and medical maggots are specially bred for use in MDT. Debridement means the surgical removal of foreign matter and dead tissue from a wound, and maggots do this by secreting their digestive juices into the wound. These liquefy the necrotic flesh which is then sucked up by the maggot. What's clever is that the enzymes in the digestive juices do not attack living tissue. In addition, the hook-like appendages on each segment of the maggot not only help the enzymes enter the tissue but also trigger chemicals which accelerate wound healing. The recommended dose is five to eight maggots per cm^2 of wound area and, because the maggots don't bite the living flesh, the patient doesn't feel any pain, only a feeling of crawling on the skin.

Which is probably what you're experiencing now.

Chilli Sauce Score: ╯

DARK VENTURE

(1956, Dir. John Calvert)

The bit where a wounded elephant leads adventurers to an elephants' graveyard

 Directed by and starring American magician and film-maker John Calvert (who celebrated his 100th birthday on 5 August 2011), this B-movie is almost as long-lost as the elephants' graveyard it contains. The film also stars John Carradine (father of the late David) as Gideon, a (shall we say) slightly peculiar guardian of the beasts' burial ground. In his day, Carradine was one of the most prolific actors in Hollywood: as well as his role in *Dark Venture*, he found time in 1956 to appear in *Around the World in Eighty Days*, *The Ten Commandments*, *The Court Jester*, *Hidden Guns* and *The Black Sleep*. But let's get back to the bones of our story.

Do elephants go to one place to die? It's actually quite hard to tell from the film, because most of the poor creatures in it are shot before they have a chance to die from natural causes in a location of their choice. However, one mortally wounded beast does make it to a sulphurous valley containing the bones of his brothers. And elephants' skeletons have indeed been found in groups, although usually near water as opposed to the film's lava-filled crater.

Studies have suggested that elephants have developed an interest in death that, within the animal kingdom, is shared only by chimpanzees. Both species display an intense fascination with the corpses of members of their groups. But when decomposition sets in, chimps lose interest and move on. Elephants, by contrast, stay. The legend of the elephants' graveyard seems to have arisen from a blurring of the animals' death fixation and the groupings of bones that have been discovered.

There are several explanations proposed as to why elephants

211

have been observed to lie down and die in a particular location. The first is down to what and how they eat. Elephants need to eat a huge amount of vegetation each day, as well as a variety of different plants and tree bark to give them the various nutrients they require. However when they are unable to ingest the necessary nutrients because of injury, illness or old age, their health goes downhill rapidly. Elephants feel the effects of malnutrition quicker than most other animals, and suffer in particular from a condition called ketosis where low blood sugar levels cause extreme lethargy. When affected, elephants stay close to water which they drink to sustain them between long periods of sleep. Eventually they die – and that's one reason why elephant remains are often found next to a body of water. Another is that, as elephants age, their teeth wear down. They can get through up to six sets in a lifetime but when the last set are worn-out they are forced to seek out the softer vegetation that tends to be found around watering holes.

When groups of elephant carcasses are discovered away from water, the cause tends to be either disease or hunting. In the days when it was legal – indeed approved of – to slaughter anything remotely wild (and the bigger the better), elephants were herded together by creating a ring of fire around them. Guns were fired, ivory plundered – and bodies simply left to decay.

So within the legend of the elephants' graveyard is buried a fair amount of truth along with the bones.

Chilli Sauce Score: ♪♪

JAWS

(1975, Dir. Steven Spielberg)

The bit where the shark attacks the boat

 If the mechanical models of the shark (all known as Bruce) hadn't been so unreliable, this watershed thriller wouldn't have scared half so many pants off half so many cinema audiences. But because the Bruces kept breaking down, Spielberg was forced to suggest rather than show the shark for much of the film. Cue yellow barrels and John Williams's relentless, menacing two-note signature tune. The film's all the more suspenseful for it, and the great white, when it appears, all the more terrifying.

Although it was actually ad-libbed by Roy Schneider, one line sums up the whole film. Schneider plays land-lubbing Police Chief Brody who, when he first comes face-to-face with the shark, mutters half in shock, "You're going to need a bigger boat." The boat in question – the Orca – is captained by Quint (Robert Shaw), a professional game-fish hunter who reckons the shark to be twenty-five feet in length (over seven metres) and three tons. But is Spielberg giving us a whopper in more senses than one?

Compared to the prehistoric megalodon shark, 'Jaws' is a tiddler. Existing between twenty and two million years ago, the megalodon is thought to have been around 15 metres long (way longer than a London bus) with a mouth that a human – had there been any around – could have walked straight into, if they'd not wanted to stay around any longer. And with teeth that were six inches long, the megalodon (meaning "big tooth" in Ancient Greek) is aptly named. It would have eaten Bruce for breakfast.

Nevertheless, the great white shark is itself the owner of some truly impressive statistics. The *Carcharodon carcharias* is referred to in the film as "an eating machine" but it could equally have been called a hunting machine, the perfect predator. Take its sense of smell, which is so important for a great white that two-thirds of its brain is devoted to it. The shark can detect some scents in a concentration of just 1 part per 25 million, which really is a drop in the ocean.

Detecting motion is also one of the great white's strong points (as opposed to playing the piano, at which they are uniformly terrible). As with most other fish, sharks detect movement via fluid-filled canals called the lateral line that run along their sides. This organ also contains hairs, which detect vibrations in the water and are sensitive enough to pick up movement from a distance of over 100 metres. And even if something isn't moving and doesn't give off a scent, the great white still knows it's there. Because sharks are able to detect the magnetic fields produced by living creatures. The ability is called electroreception and involves pores on the shark's head which contain small cells called ampullae of Lorenzini. These cells hold a gel-like substance that conducts electricity. Each cell also contains a tiny hair which, when electricity passes through the gel, transmits a signal to the fish's brain. Such is the sensitivity of the great white's electroreception ability that it's as perceptive and precise as the most sophisticated man-made devices.

And they do get big. Six metres long with a weight of 2000 kg represents the generally-agreed maximum size of a great white. However as with many other fishing claims, the largest great white of all is a matter for conjecture and disputation. Even the *Guinness Book of World Records* has got in on the act, for years listing a 12.6 m beast caught off the Azores as the biggest of all. However the listing is no longer, er, listed. The largest shark which has been reliably measured was one caught by six Cuban fishermen in 1945. It came in at just over 6.4 metres and weighed a truly astonishing 3.2 tons. What's even more remarkable was that the fishermen were crammed into a four-metre-long wooden skiff at the time. But the ocean's a big place and many aspects

of the great white and its behaviour are yet to be observed. So perhaps there's an even bigger "Jaws" just waiting to be found.

That's if you're not too scared to go into the water.

Chilli Sauce Score: ♪

CRIME

"I may not know much of law, Mr Felder, but I know what's right and what's wrong."

Young Mr. Lincoln

SEVEN

(1995, Dir. David Fincher)

The bit where Kevin Spacey cuts the skin from his fingers so he won't leave prints

 Heaven help you if you were lustful, lazy, liked to stuff your face and lived anywhere near Kevin Spacey's creepy psychopath, John Doe. As likely as not, you'd have ended up carving off a pound of your own flesh, strapped to a bed for a year or dying face-down in a bowl of spaghetti. Even if you yourself had managed to steer clear of the seven deadly sins, your other half could well have found themselves with their head lopped off.

So how did Doe keep the cops away for so long? The crazy S.O.B. sliced the skin from his digits so he wouldn't leave fingerprints, that's how.

The real-life U.S. Federal Bureau of Investigation tackles printless wrong-uns like John Doe in their *Taking Legible Fingerprints* manual, which states, "If the individual has a bandage or cast on a finger, thumb or hand, place the notation, 'Unable to Print' or 'UP' in the appropriate finger block". But they've still got to catch him first. Doe knew that fingerprints grow back unless you keep cutting off the skin.

He's not the only one. More than a few migrants looking to find their way to Britain from Calais are reported to have heated up metal bolts before touching the white-hot metal with their fingers. Said one young man from Kenya, "I have to do this regularly because your prints can grow back." The reason for this desperate self-mutilation is that migrants can be deported if their fingerprints reveal they have already lodged asylum applications. Without fingerprints, checks can't be made.

Even more gruesomely, in 2008 in Mexico a plastic surgeon was jailed for 18 months for replacing the fingerprints of a drug dealer with skin from the bottom of his feet (the drug dealer's feet not his own, I presume). So erasing one's fingerprints does seem to be an accepted way of trying to evade the authorities.

However the fact that all the above singularly failed to evade the authorities suggests there's often a lot of pain for scant gain.

Chilli Sauce Score:)

THE DAY OF THE JACKAL

(1973, Dir. Fred Zinnemann)

The bit where the Jackal swallows cordite to age his skin

 Edward Fox's Jackal may have ended up being lowered into the ground in a coffin, but while he was alive and on a mission to kill President Charles de Gaulle, there was no hitman more efficient or ruthless. A consummate professional, the Jackal goes to extraordinary lengths to conceal his identity and change his appearance, including swallowing cordite to make his skin turn a rather sickly grey.

First, what is cordite? It's a type of military propellant – now obsolete – that was developed in England towards the end of the nineteenth century to replace gunpowder. It consists of 58% nitroglycerine, 37% guncotton and 5% vaseline, and was formed into thin rods called cord powder – hence cordite. In the film we learn that if you swallow a couple of pieces of cordite you feel sick and your skin turns grey. Then after about an hour, you feel well again but your skin remains grey and you're ready to go kill a head of state.

The real-life effects of cordite exposure were observed and reported in a 1947 experiment. It seems that cordite makes you feel a bit worse than just "sick". And this was when subjects of the experiment were merely in the same room as the cordite, rather than wolfing it down. The report states that most of the subjects suffered from a headache, the main characteristics of which "were its severity and its frontal situation. With time the headache often spread to the vertex… one individual said it 'lifted the top of his head off'. In many cases the headache stopped for a while during the trial but returned later, usually on leaving the trial room, and persisted a variable time up to twenty-four hours. When severe there were symptoms of nausea, and in several cases there were complaints of abdominal pain." Pleasant stuff, then.

The report doesn't make any mention of changes to skin colour. However the symptoms of a nitroglycerin overdose (nitroglycerin being the main constituent of cordite) are a bluish colour to lips and fingernails, and cold skin. So here we have the skin changing colour (blue's pretty close to grey, I guess). The trouble is that these symptoms are pretty much indistinguishable from those associated with death.

For grey skin with added survival, we can turn to the former Ukrainian President Viktor Yushchenko, who was mysteriously poisoned in 2004. The toxin used was not cordite but dioxin, but it did cause Yushchenko's face to become covered with grey warts – the closest we get to the Jackal's poisonous ploy.

The warts on their own might have been enough to scare de Gaulle to death.

Chilli Sauce Score:))))

KEYSTONE HOTEL

(1935, Dir. Ralph Staub)

The bit where a custard pie is teleported down a phone line

Like a silent comedy but with sound, this slapstick short pays homage to the earlier Keystone comedies produced by Mack Sennett. A beauty pageant is held at the Keystone Hotel and the cross-eyed judge awards first prize to an elderly cleaning woman. A riot ensues but, this being slapstick, instead of chairs being hurled it's custard pies, in what could well be the best pie fight in film history. One pie even gets thrown down a phone receiver and hits the person on the other end of the line. Teleportation may well have been a pipe dream (incidentally, a phrase derived from the fantasies of opium smokers) in 1935. But what about today?

The method of transport favoured by *Star Trek*'s Captain Kirk and crew involves someone or something dematerializing at one location before their exact atomic configuration is beamed to another location and then reassembled. And for most of the 20th century, it was a concept that was confined to the anything-goes worlds of slapstick and science fiction. But in 1993 Charles Bennett, a physicist at IBM, proved that teleportation was theoretically possible. However he tempered his discovery with the caveat that the original object being teleported would be destroyed. Five years later Bennett's theory became reality when physicists at the California Institute of Technology managed to teleport a photon (the particle of energy that carries light) across a distance of one metre. However three photons were actually needed to achieve teleportation: the photon to be teleported, a transporting photon and a receiving photon all acting together in a process called quantum entanglement. Also, the teleportation didn't occur

through the air but along one metre of coaxial cable. Hmmm. Could be a while before they get a custard pie down that cable.

A more recent experiment took place in 2006 at the Niels Bohr Institute in Copenhagen, when scientists successfully teleported information stored in a laser beam into a cloud of atoms half a metre away. With one type of matter being transmitted into the midst of another type, this was much closer to the Kirk-onto-a-planet teleportation that cinema audiences are familiar with. Yet with all teleportation experiments so far, the object being teleported hasn't actually dematerialized and then rematerialized somewhere else. Instead, as in a fax machine, the original is duplicated in another location. And actual human (or for that matter custard pie) teleportation is a long way off. For that to happen, a machine would have to analyse and map the trillion trillion atoms that make up your body. It would then have to send all this information to another location. With today's best optical fibres, this would take roughly a hundred million centuries to do. Then your trillion trillion atoms would have to be perfectly reconstructed, or you might end up with a leg protruding from your forehead.

But there may be another way: via wormholes. These theoretical rifts in space could (in theory) teleport a person somewhere else in an instant. However (there's always a "however") the forces involved are similar to those in a black hole. Anyone foolish enough to enter a wormhole would be stretched until they were very long and very thin, a process that scientists call (in a refreshing instance of non-jargon) *spaghettification*.

So teleportation might just happen in the future, but for today's cinema audiences it's definitely a leap of faith.

Chilli Sauce Score: ♪♪♪♪

YOUNG MR. LINCOLN

(1939, Dir. John Ford)

The bit where Abe bites a coin to test whether it's fake

They're big shoes to fill: the 16th President of The United States, preserver of the Union, deliverer of the Gettysburg Address and pioneer of the abolition of slavery. Perhaps that's why Henry Fonda wore special shoes to make him appear taller. In fact, Fonda gives one of the best performances of his early career in this first of seven films he made with one of the greatest of all American directors, John Ford.

Young Mr. Lincoln is a fictionalized account of Lincoln as a novice lawyer, struggling with his first real case – a murder. The president-to-be displays many president-to-be qualities: honour, compassion… and the ability to spot when a farmer is fobbing him off with a fake gold coin. Lincoln bites the coin to see if it's actually made from gold. But does this actually work?

Gold has been used for ornamentation and rituals since pre-historic times. It's been depicted in the hieroglyphs of Egypt (where it was believed to be an indestructible metal of the gods) and appears in the Old Testament. In the 14th century B.C., King Tushratta of the Mitanni (in Syria) claimed it was as "common as dust" – lucky him. Elsewhere, gold has been called "the sweat of the sun" (the Incas) and "the excrement of the gods" (the Aztecs).

The metal was used in what was probably the world's first coinage in Lydia (in modern Turkey) in the 7th century B.C. Skip forward to Venice in the year 1284 and the gold ducat was introduced, becoming the most popular coin in the world. In the same year, Great Britain issued its first major gold coin, the florin. In 1511 King Ferdinand of Spain launched his country's military expeditions with the instruction: "Get gold, humanely if you can, but all hazards, get gold." And in 1700 Master of the Mint Sir Isaac

Newton fixed the price of gold in Great Britain at 84 shillings, 11.5 pence per troy ounce, a price that lasted for over 200 years. (A troy ounce is one of the units of mass used for precious metals, gunpowder and gemstones. It's named after Troyes in France and is equivalent to 31.1034768 grams.)

One fateful day in 1848, John Marshall found flakes of gold while building a sawmill in California. The California Gold Rush followed, bringing in its wake the rapid settlement of the American West. By the 20th century, applications for gold had gone from the purely decorative and monetary to the hi-tech and extraterrestrial, including being used in the engine compartment of McLaren's F1 supercar and on the visors of astronauts to help protect their eyes from the sun.

It's been calculated that 165,000 tonnes of gold have been excavated since the beginning of time and, because of its durability, as much as 85 per cent is still in circulation. At first glance, 165,000 tonnes may seem like a lot of gold. But if it was all collected and moulded into a cube, the cube would only measure 20 metres by 20 metres by 20 metres. *That's all the gold ever mined.* So perhaps it isn't surprising that the history of real gold is also littered with countless attempts to fake it. Brass has been used, so too has lead. Even nature has had a go with pyrite, known as fool's gold.

Back to the bite test and whether it's a good test of gold's authenticity. You won't find many goldsmiths sinking their teeth into your late granny's jewellery, but biting is actually not a bad way to discover whether your next holiday is going to be in Barbados or Bognor. Gold is a soft metal and does indeed yield when bitten. However, nowadays gold leaf can be applied thinly over other soft metals such as lead. So other checks are used, including nitric acid, which makes metals other than gold discolour to green.

But at the time when *Young Mr. Lincoln* was set, biting gold was an acceptable test, not a 24-carat Hollywood lie.

Chilli Sauce Score:)

THE TOWN

(2010, Dir. Ben Affleck)

The bit where Boston has the most dangerous neighbourhood in the world

 Ben Affleck used to be thought by many to be a bit of an ass. Much of it was probably envy. After all, he bagged an Oscar for *Good Will Hunting* when he was only twenty-four, before bagging (if only temporarily) Jennifer Lopez. And some of it was undoubtedly a reaction to Affleck's participation in such nonsense as *Armageddon*, *Surviving Christmas* and *Jersey Girl*. But underneath the all-American handsomeness there lies a seriously talented filmmaker, both in front of and behind the camera.

Take *The Town*, which could so easily have ended up being a run-of-the-mill crime drama. Instead Affleck's second directorial outing (in which he also stars) is tense, dynamic and superbly-acted. The film is set in Charlestown in the city of Boston, Massachusetts. But is this one mile-square area really as dangerous as the film's title card suggests when it claims that "One blue-collar Boston neighborhood has produced more bank robbers and armored car thieves than anywhere in the world"?

It's a fair bet that anyone who was trying to sell their house in Charlestown when the film was released would have been more than a little annoyed to read that. Who's going to want to move to an area where people experience bank robberies as often as other people experience dinner? Up to the mid-1990s, though, Charlestown was indeed known for the number of bank robbers who congregated there. What about now? The FBI record sbank robberies by state rather than by neighbourhood and, in the first quarter of 2010, there were 23 bank robberies in the whole of Massachusetts compared to 49 in Illinois and 136 in California.

So if Charlestown did used to have an abundance of criminals, they seem to have moved on to pastures new. Pastures like the top ten most dangerous cities in the world.

These places have been rated for their all-round nastiness, and all-round nasty they are too. In tenth place is the city of Muzaffarabad which, because it lies in the disputed region of Kashmir, could well be in the firing line if things get nuclear between Pakistan and India. Aside from the threat of being wiped from the map, Muzaffarabad also suffers from corruption, abductions, political violence, drug and human trafficking.

Ninth is Santo Domingo, the capital of the Dominican Republic, and a city in which they treat tourists exactly the same way that they treat their own people: they mug them. Eighth is Grozny, the capital of the Chechen Republic in Russia. Grozny was given the dubious accolade of "The Most Destroyed City on Earth" by the UN in 2003. Things haven't improved much and gangsters run riot through what is left of Grozny, with very high rates of kidnapping, rape and murder.

Port Moresby, the capital of Papua New Guinea, comes next. If you don't suffer a carjacking, your vehicle will probably be stoned. If you're not pickpocketed, it'll be armed robbery. Papua New Guinea is also situated in an active seismic zone, so tsunamis, earthquakes and landslides add to the fun. In sixth place is Caracas in Venezuela. Criminal activity begins at the airport where corruption is common. The murder rate is one of the highest in the world. Express kidnappings, where people are snatched for quick cash are also popular. But don't call the cops because they're often involved.

Fifth is Mogadishu in Somalia, where rival militias battle it out on a daily basis with little regard for anyone else. If you're not caught in cross-fire, the street criminals will get you instead. Port-au-Prince, the capital of Haiti comes fourth. Many people think that the 2010 earthquake was the source of all Haiti's problems. But the UN has been trying to help police the country since 2004.

Haiti is one of the four most important countries for drug transit to the US. And Port-au-Prince leads the way in murders, gun battles and robberies.

We're into the top three now. Third is St. Louis in Missouri, which has been pronounced "America's Most Dangerous City" thanks to its FBI-collated statistics for murder, rape, robbery and assault. In comparison to a national average of 429.4, St. Louis has 2,070.1 violent crimes per 100,000 residents (it should be said that this rating is highly contested, especially by those who live in St Louis). In second place is Ciudad Juárez in Mexico. It's been called "the most violent zone in the world outside of declared war zones". There were 1,400 murders in Ciudad Juárez in 2008. In 2010 there were over 2,500 drug-related deaths. And over the past 10 years, 400 women have been killed in sexual homicides.

But first place goes to... Bogotá, the capital of Colombia. Narco-terrorism is the thing here, giving the city one of the highest violent crime rates in the world. Bombings, carjacking, kidnapping – if it's nasty and it ends in "ing" it's likely that you'll fall victim to it in Bogotá.

All of which makes Charlestown look like Chelsea.

Chilli Sauce Score: ♪♪♪♪

THE STING

(1973, Dir. George Roy Hill)

The bit where Paul Newman cheats at poker

A film with a My-God-did-that-really-happen twist at its end. On second thoughts, if you haven't seen the film it's probably best you don't even know that the end has a twist. So, do a Leonard Shelby (remember? The one with amnesia in *Memento*) and forget I mentioned it. What you ought to know is that *The Sting* is an immensely enjoyable yarn about con artists in 1930s America. And Paul Newman and Robert Redford do indeed turn the confidence trick into an art form, pulling the trickiest of tricks on crime boss Robert Shaw.

The film is divided into seven sections, each with its own title. "The Hook" concerns Henry Gondorff (Newman) getting Doyle Lonnegan (Shaw) to take the bait that will eventually lead him to fall victim to a much larger sting. The bait takes the form of a high-stake poker game aboard a train from New York to Chicago. Gondorff, posing as a drunken and boorish bookie, is actually a highly-skilled cardsharp and manages to relieve Shaw of $15,000. It's an impressive display of card playing, especially as Lonnegan is cheating and believes he's got the game sewn up. But Gondorff has one last trick up his sleeve, and somehow manages to swap the four nines in his hand for four jacks. But is the director cheating us too?

In one survey, over 50% of poker players admitted to cheating. So there are obviously ways and means. However, as the average poker game consists of a few friends and a lot of booze at somebody's house, cheating methods are probably no more sophisticated that asking an opponent to fetch a beer while you take a sneaky peak at their cards. Henry Gondorff is a different kettle of fish entirely. He's a card shark, a professional. A shark

turns cheating at poker into a sophisticated operation. He chooses his victims, his method and his moment. And bang! When a shark cheats, his opponents won't know what's hit them. That's if they know they've been hit at all.

The poker game in the film shows some tricksy dealing by Gondorff (some of the close-ups show a professional card player's hands). One of the moves is called a second deal, where the player secretly deals the second rather than the top card from the pack. This in itself isn't enough to achieve the kind of grand switch pulled off by Gondorff at the end of the game. However, there are various card-cheating accessories that sharks have been known to use which can dramatically alter the outcome of a game. Some are called holdout devices, and enable a player to "hold out" a card or cards from the game until they are required. In fact, holding only one card out of play can dramatically increase a player's chances of compiling a winning hand, as he or she can introduce it whenever they want whilst also knowing that no other player can be dealt the card.

Most holdout devices were invented in the 19th century and range from simple gadgets to complex machines requiring a high level of skill to operate. The simpler devices include one that enables a player to clip a card to the underside of the table, and one that consists of a secret pocket on the underside of a player's sleeve. One known as the short-sleeve holdout – which is worn on the bicep underneath a short-sleeved shirt and which, with a bit of arm crossing, allows a shark to secrete and retrieve cards at will – can be made from nothing more than a rubber band, a paperclip and a piece of folded paper.

Things get a bit more complicated with mechanical apparatus known as arm-pressure sleeve holdouts, which use levers, springs and pulleys – and a bit more comical with devices sewn into the clothes and known as vest holdouts, pants holdouts and the wonderfully-named knee-spread holdouts. There are even machines called deck switchers that do just that, as well as whole

card tables designed to conceal extra cards and help the shark make a killing. So with the right equipment, skill and *cojones*, it may just be possible to swap four nines for four jacks. But as with all sharks, the real trick is not to get caught.

Chilli Sauce Score: ♩♩

OUR DARE-DEVIL CHIEF

(1915, Dir. Charley Chase)

The bit where a paper plane sticks in the mayor's chest

The oldest film in this book is a Mack Sennett-produced Keystone caper. A city mayor is having a rough time. Not only does his wife seem to fancy the chief of police, but a gang of thieves wants to blow him up. At least they are thoughtful enough to send him a note saying they're going to kill him. The note is folded into a paper aeroplane and thrown through a window, hitting the mayor in the chest and sticking there. But isn't a paper aeroplane (like the scenario) just a bit too flimsy?

When scale is taken into account, a normal sheet of paper is actually as strong as aircraft-grade aluminium. And when you also consider that some enthusiasts use Computer-Aided Design (CAD) software to develop their paper planes, it becomes clear there's more to it than a few folds, a throw, a loop-the-loop and a crash landing at your feet. The current record holder for the longest flight in terms of time is Takuo Toda, president of the Japanese Origami Aeroplane Association. In April 2009 at a competition in Hiroshima, Toda's 10cm-long plane, made from a single sheet of paper, stayed aloft for 27.9 seconds. However this was something of a hollow triumph for the President, because his record-breaking plane incorporated some sellotape – anathema to origima purists.

So in December 2009, Toda decided to stick (without using sellotape) to the principles of origami proper, and fashioned a plane from a single piece of paper and nothing else. This he lobbed into the air, where it remained for 26.1 seconds before landing. According to Toda the key to a long and successful flight is all in the throwing technique. The main objective is to get the plane as high as possible into the air so that it can circle slowly

back down again. Indeed some enthusiasts manage to throw their planes at nearly 100 km/h to a height of some 18 metres.

Toda is now on a mission to break the half-minute flight mark and seems confident. "I will get the 30-second record," he said. "It's just a matter of time." He's also involved in plans to have a Japanese astronaut launch 100 paper planes from the International Space Station, 250 miles above Earth. Test planes have been modelled using silicon-coated, heat-resistant paper and have survived practice temperatures of 250°C and wind speeds of seven times the speed of sound. However since there is no way to track the planes on their week-long journey back to Earth, Toda's plans, and planes, have yet to get off the ground.

Perhaps he should lower his sights just a little, as a paper aeroplane has in fact already made it into space. It was "launched" using a helium balloon in November 2010 by a team of British amateur space enthusiasts. Having reached a height of nearly 30 km above sea level, the balloon burst and the plane drifted back down to Earth. It even carried a camera which took pictures during its 90-minute descent. And in a triumph of British amateurism over Japanese sophistication, the plane was constructed from nothing more than paper straws, covered in paper.

Back to *Our Dare-Devil Chief*. It looks as though the crook's paper plane might well have had sufficient force to become lodged in the mayor's uniform.

At least, on paper.

Chilli Sauce Score:

FIGHT CLUB

(1999, Dir. David Fincher)

The bit where a napalm bomb is made from gasoline and orange juice

 The first rule of Fight Club is... you don't do what everyone else does and recite the first rule of Fight Club. Especially when this controversial, brutally entertaining film contains so many other quotable quotes: "Sticking feathers up your butt does not make you a chicken"... "Is that your blood?" "Some of it, yeah"... "If you could fight anyone, who would you fight?" "Shatner. I'd fight William Shatner." Edward Norton is the insomniac office worker taking lessons in mayhem from Brad Pitt's anarchic soap salesman and learning that napalm can apparently be made from gasoline and frozen orange juice.

Few weapons are as notorious as napalm. Its use in World War II and, in particular, in Vietnam has left the world with images of firestorms and screaming children, skin hanging from their bodies like rags. Napalm was first developed in 1942 by Harvard researchers working with the US military. Before that time, the fires caused by incendiary bombs and devices such as flamethrowers burned out relatively quickly. But that changed when the researchers mixed an aluminium soap powder of naphthalene with palmitate (a type of fatty acid) to make a jelly they called napalm. Tey then combined the napalm with gasoline to produce a substance that would stick to anything it touched and then burn for a prolonged period of time to cause maximum damage.

Fair enough if you're trying to destroy an enemy position in the heat of battle. But when napalm comes into contact with skin, the effects can be truly horrific. Everyone's heard of first, second and third degree burns, which range from injury to the outer skin (epidermis) to injury to the inner layer of inner skin (known as the dermis). Napalm can cause what are unofficially referred to as fourth degree burns – burns which reach beneath the skin to destroy tissue, muscles, ligaments and bones. (The pain from fourth degree burns is so excruciating that people have died from it alone.) And if that weren't enough, napalm bombing can result in a number of unpleasant secondary effects. Large amounts of carbon monoxide are produced when a napalm bomb is detonated, causing severe breathing difficulties as well as longer-term carbon monoxide poisoning and disturbances of the nervous system. Napalm casualties can also suffer from burnt windpipes, abnormal bone growth and overwhelming shock, as a result of being caught up in a hellish firestorm with self-perpetuating and searing windstorms of up to 110 km/h.

Modern-day napalm, called Napalm B, is not napalm at all but a mixture of 46 parts polystyrene, 33 parts gasoline and 21 parts benzene. This combination is much harder to ignite than the original napalm (you could throw a grenade into it and it wouldn't catch fire) and is therefore considered "safer" – though of course those on the receiving end of a Napalm B bomb would not comsider it particularly safe.

Can napalm be made from gasoline and frozen orange juice? Fortunately not, as the ingredients in the Napalm recipe were changed in the film to ensure that any nutters in the audience wouldn't immediately pop down to their 24-hour petrol station to fill up on bomb-making ingredients. The real ingredients are as detailed above.

But combining them really is a recipe for disaster.

Chilli Sauce Score: $\mathcal{J} \mathcal{J} \mathcal{J} \mathcal{J}$

LIFE OF BRIAN

(1979, Dir. Terry Jones)

The bit where Brian bears his cross

Blasphemy – no; parody – oh yes. The Pythons (or rather Terry Jones in a dress) explicitly state that Brian is not the Messiah, just "a very naughty boy". Born on Christmas day in a stable next door to a baby named Jesus, Brian Cohen is mistaken for the son of God and has to suffer the attentions of the local Judaeans, who hang on his every word (and covet his every sandal), and the Romans, who overcome their innate incompetence and pwepostewous pwonunciation long enough to sentence Brian to death. Before he is crucified, Brian and his fellow prisoners have to carry their crosses up to the place of their execution. But wouldn't a cross be far too heavy to lift?

Brian's cross appears to be made of particularly flimsy pieces of wood, but outside the Gospels accounts of crucifixion are thin on the ground. Lucius Annaeus Seneca (4 B.C. – 65 A.D.) mentions one mass crucifixion, recording that "I see crosses there, not just of one kind but made in many different ways: some have their victims with their head down to the ground, some impale their private parts, others stretch out their arms." But there are no surviving instructions detailing how to perform a crucifixion, or setting out the ideal size and proportions for the cross.

What is evident is that crosses and crucifixions took a variety of forms. However if the thick wooden beams depicted in centuries of art (as opposed to a few minutes of Python) are a fair representation of reality, it's clear that a whole cross would be very heavy indeed – probably in the region of 150 kg. This would make it impossible for all but the most beefy condemned person to carry or even drag it to the place of their execution. Instead they would probably have been forced to carry the crossbeam,

which would have weighed a more bearable 50 kilos. The Roman historian Tacitus (56 – 117 A.D.) wrote that the city of Rome had a specific area for crucifixions outside the Esquiline Gate. And it could well have been the case that the upright posts were permanently positioned there, meaning the prisoners only needed to carry their crossbeams to the Gate. Lucky them.

Because the bodies of most crucified people were thrown to the dogs or out with the rubbish, there is very little surviving archaeological evidence of crucifixions. There is one case however, that of a young Jewish man who lived and then was killed in Palestine during Roman times. When his bones were unearthed recently, scientists were permitted to analyse them for a short time before the remains were given a Jewish burial. In that time an 11.5 cm iron nail was discovered piercing the man's heel bone. A flat piece of olive wood was also found between the head of the nail and the bone, which may have been placed there to stop the man pulling his foot off the nail. There was, however, no evidence that the man's wrists or hands had been nailed to a cross – nor indeed of the existence of a cross.

So there are few indisputable facts concerning crucifixion. Yet it is safe to assume that it must have been very hard indeed to look on the bright side of life.

Chilli Sauce Score: 𝄐 𝄐 𝄐

THE SILENCE OF THE LAMBS

(1991, Dir. Jonathan Demme)

The bit where Hannibal wears someone else's face

Anthony Hopkins, playing Dr Hannibal Lecter (handy to be a flesh-eating serial killer and to have a name that rhymes with cannibal), is only on screen for sixteen minutes. But those small doses of menace are what make the film so thrilling (and explain why the sequels aren't). Lecter's restricted screen time also makes his escape particularly unnerving, not least when he carves the skin off a policeman's face to use as a disguise. But can someone's face actually be removed in one piece and worn by somebody else?

Removing the skin from a person's face in its entirety can be done. Lecter uses a knife and, because he only wants to "wear" the police officer's face rather than actually transplant it, he accomplishes the feat in a few minutes. Transplant surgeons, on the other hand, take more time and care during a four-hour operation in which skin, veins, arteries, muscles and bones are all carefully removed from the (dead) donor's face.

Accidents can also result in a literal loss of face. For instance, a person's hair can get caught in machinery, which then tears the scalp and sometimes the whole face from the head. This has happened to a woman in Australia, to a man in the United States who got his hair caught in a conveyer belt, and to a nine year-old Indian girl called Sandeep Kaur.

In 1994 Sandeep was chopping grass for the family buffalo when her hair became caught in a threshing machine. Her entire face and scalp were torn off. Her family put Sandeep's face in a bag and rode her on a moped to the nearest medical centre, three and a half hours away. Surgeons decided that skin grafts would leave Sandeep horribly disfigured and so they chose instead to perform

the world's first full face reattachment. Happily for Sandeep, the operation went well, with only a small amount of scarring, and she has able to lead a normal life ever since.

The operation's success was partly due to the fact that the surgeons were reattaching Sandeep's original skin, rather than transplanting a donor's face. It wasn't until 2010 that a full-face transplant would be achieved. The recipient, a Spanish man known only as Oscar, lost his jaw, nose and other parts of his face in a shooting accident. A team of thirty doctors rebuilt his face in a 22-hour operation, using a donor's entire facial skin, muscles, nose, cheekbones, jawbone and even teeth, with metal plates being used to support the new facial structure and to reconstruct the roof of the mouth.

The donor's face and accompanying nerves and blood vessels were stitched to Oscar using advanced microvascular techniques, although he will have to take anti-rejection drugs for the rest of his life. Like other patients who have had varying degrees of face transplants, Oscar neither looks like his donor nor his original self, but somewhere in between. This, of course, is because a person's appearance isn't just down to their skin but also the underlying bone structure. And that's the problem with *The Silence of the Lambs*. Just cutting the skin off someone's face and plonking it on top of his own wouldn't have made Hannibal look like the person, which is how he is supposed to have been able to effect his escape.

Does it matter? Of course not – especially as most people watching the film have their eyes shut at this point.

Chilli Sauce Score: ♪♪♪

THE ITALIAN JOB

(1969, Dir. Peter Collinson)

The bit where Michael Caine has a great idea

How better to end than, literally, on a cliffhanger? The credits roll and we never find out whether Charlie Croker (Caine) manages to remove the gold which is stuck at one end of the coach, with his gang trapped at the other. One false move and coach, gold and gang would teeter over the edge to be smashed to smithereens on the rocks below. So what could the idea have been, and would it have worked?

Caine actually revealed his version of the idea in 2009: "I crawl up, switch on the engine and stay there for four hours until all the petrol runs out," said Sir Michael. "The coach bounces back up so we can all get out, but then the gold goes over. There is a load of Corsican Mafia at the bottom watching the whole thing with binoculars. They grab the gold and then the sequel is us chasing it." Now we know what the idea was. But is it plausible? A gold bar weighs 23 kg, so 77 bars weigh one ton. And there appear to be many more than that on the coach. So it would have required a careful balancing act to get gold and geezers back on terra firma. Handily, in 2008 (a year before Caine's revelation) the Royal Society of Chemistry announced a competition to solve the conundrum by working out a plausible way of removing the gold before the coach tips over. Submissions were required to be based on the principles of serious scientific investigation. And judges were instructed not to accept any solutions that involve the use of a helicopter. (Spoilsports!)

In fact the winning suggestion (out of 2,000 submitted) was similar to Caine's version, in that it involved getting rid of the vehicle's fuel. John Godwin from Surrey proposed that the first thing to do would be to stabilise the coach by smashing out the

windows on the part of the coach overlooking the drop, with the glass falling into the ravine below. Then the windows at the end of the coach perched on the cliff-top could be smashed inward to improve the weight ratio slightly. Next, one of the gang would be lowered outside the coach to deflate its tyres and stop the vehicle from rocking. After that, the weight distribution could be improved further by emptying the fuel tank, which Godwin found out was at the rear of the coach (the end containing the gold and overhanging the ravine). Godwin estimated the tank would contain 140 kg of fuel – nearly the weight of two men. The draining of the fuel would allow a member of the gang to leave the overhanging end of the coach and bring rocks back to put inside the coach at the cliff-top end, thus weighing it down enough for the gold to be safely removed.

So it turns out that Sir Michael's great idea was, indeed, just the job.

Chilli Sauce Score: ♩

FURTHER READING

The Self-Transcendence 3100 Mile Race: www.3100.ws
Check Jesper's progress at www.worldrun.org

Human magnetism: www.slate.com/id/2185455/

Website dedicated to Weissmuller: www.geostan.ca
The Edgar Rice Burrows webzine: www.erbzine.com

Report on trepanation: http://news.bbc.co.uk/1/hi/uk/461556.stm
The International Trepanation Advisory Group: www.trepan.com
The history of the lobotomy: http://psychcentral.com/blog/
    archives/2011/03/21/the-surprising-history-of-the-lobotomy/
The Hemispherectomy Foundation: http://hemifoundation.
    intuitwebsites.com
Mike the Headless Chicken: www.miketheheadlesschicken.org

Freediving: www.britishfreediving.org
www.aida-international.org
Report on Merlini: www.formula1.com/news/
    headlines/2009/4/9274.html

Defining genius: http://people.howstuffworks.com/genius.htm
www.mensa.org
www.faqs.org/faqs/mensa/faq/

Psychophysical and Behavioral Characteristics of Olfactory
    Adaptation by Pamela Dalton, quoted at www.chemse.
    oxfordjournals.org/cgi/content/full/25/4/487
The Sense of Smell Institute: www.senseofsmell.org

All things red: www.raising-redheads.com/index.html

245

http://news.bbc.co.uk/1/hi/6725653.stm
www.purgatory.net/kornelia/1603/red_hair_facts.htm

Article on the thermal conductivity of metal at the Cornell
    Centre for Materials Research website: www.ccmr.cornell.
    edu/education/ask/index.html?quid=777

"Unhappy Meal. How to eat yourself to death." by Marry Roach at
    www.salon.com/health/col/roac/1999/12/03/roach/index.html
Article on python and alligator: http://news.bbc.co.uk/1/
    hi/4313978.stm

Memory Loss at the Movies by Daniel Pendick at www.
    memorylossonline.com/spring2002/memlossatmovies.htm
Memories Aren't Made of This: Amnesia at the Movies by Sallie
    Baxendale
at www.bmj.com/cgi/content/long/329/7480/1480
Obituary of Henry Molaison: www.telegraph.co.uk/news/
    obituaries/4109336/Henry-Molaison.html

Ron Perlman fansite and review of The Name of the Rose: http://
    www.perlmanpages.com/bsmovies/nameroserev.htm
Article on glossolalia study: http://www.nytimes.
    com/2006/11/07/health/07brain.html

Information on pain and its suppression: www.
    britishpainsociety.org
www.bbc.co.uk/news/health-12297569
The boy who can't feel pain: http://news.bbc.co.uk/1/hi/
    health/4195437.stm
Steven and Paul's website: www.thefactsofpainlesspeople.com

The Descent of Man, and Selection in Relation to Sex by Charles
    Darwin (first published 1871)
The Record Setter website: www.recordsetter.com

The naughty version of Edward's chair: www.dailymail.co.uk/
    news/article-1259670/A-love-seat-fit-king-The-antique-chair-
    gives-eye-popping-insight-Edward-VIIs-debauched-youth.
    html
The proper version: http://medievalnews.blogspot.com/2010/04/
    englands-700-year-old-coronation-chair.html
http://news.scotsman.com/uk/200000--bill-for-
    conservation.6238272.jp
www.westminster-abbey.org/visit-us/highlights/the-coronation-
    chair

Information on the history and types of matches at
http://everything2.com/title/Strike+Anywhere+matches
http://www.wisegeek.com/what-are-strike-anywhere-matches.
    htm

A history of lenses and telescopes: www.optics1.com/optics_
    history.php

Information on and history of nitrate film courtesy of Roger
    Smither, Keeper, Film and Photograph Archives at the
    Imperial War Museum and Editor of This Film is Dangerous:
    A Celebration of Nitrate Film (2002, FIAF Brussels)

Article on the British Film Institute: www.timeout.com/film/
    features/show-feature/3302/inside-the-bfi.html

Information on fire fighting and equipment: www.cambsfire.gov.
    uk and www.fireservice.co.uk

Some of the world's biggest Christmas light displays:
www.digsdigs.com/top-10-biggest-outdoor-christmas-lights-
   house-decorations/

Examples of glasses wearing on TV and film: http://tvtropes.org/
   pmwiki/pmwiki.php/Main/BrainySpecs
The link between glasses and intelligence: www.infoniac.com/
   science/people-wearing-glasses-more-intelligent.html
Reports on 'intelligent' glasses: www.dailymail.co.uk/news/
   article-533358/The-Smart-Goggles-make-lost-keys-mobile-
   phones-iPod-thing-past.html

Only one source is required for everything to do with turn-
   of-the-century magic, the superb Hiding the Elephant:
   How Magicians Invented the Impossible by Jim Steinmeyer
   (Carroll & Graf, 2004).

History of the bowler: http://www.telegraph.co.uk/news/
   uknews/8045026/History-of-the-Bowler-Hat.html
History of the Plug Uglies: http://www.associatepublisher.
   com/e/p/pl/plug_uglies.htm

Experts shed light on mirrors: http://science.howstuffworks.
   com/innovation/everyday-innovations/mirror.htm www.
   explainthatstuff.com/howmirrorswork.html

Premature burials: http://listverse.com/2010/02/02/10-
   horrifying-premature-burials/
Safety coffin designs: http://www.ehow.co.uk/info_8139414_
   were-bells-put-coffins.html
How to survive being buried in The Complete Worst Case
   Scenario Survival Handbook by Joshua Piven and David
   Borgenicht (Chronicle Books, 2007)

Roald Dahl's obituary: www.thisisannouncements.
co.uk/5848795

The myth debunked by someone who works for the Canadian
Forest Service: www.angelfire.com/folk/slcannex/debunk_
scuba.htm

The Canadian drive-in twister story debunked: www.snopes.
com/movies/films/twister.asp
A real-life storm chaser's website: www.stormchase.com
The British-based Tornado and Storm Research Organisation:
www.torro.org.uk

Tumbleweed facts: www.absoluteastronomy.com/topics/
Tumbleweed

Information on meteors: www.solarviews.com/eng/meteor.htm
Article on space trash: www.metro.co.uk/news/
newsfocus/658425-friend-foe-or-astronaut-s-fridge

Information on the film St. Elmo's Fire: www.imdb.com/title/
tt0090060/
The history and science of the phenomenon: www.islandnet.
com/~see/weather/elements/stelmo.htm

The physics of quicksand: www.damninteresting.com/the-
physics-of-quicksand

What makes an echo: www.physicsclassroom.com/Class/sound/
u11l3d.cfm www.worsleyschool.net/science/files/echo/echo.
html

Information on tasers: www.taser.com

Information on electric shocks: www.allaboutcircuits.com/vol_1/chpt_3/2.html

Information on defibrillation: http://en.wikipedia.org/wiki/Defibrillator

Information on arc flashes: http://arcflash.com.au/

The role of the moon in the film: www.film.com/features/story/300-changes-the-cgi-game/13813411

Moon facts: http://nssdc.gsfc.nasa.gov/planetary/planets/moonpage.html

The moon illusion: http://news.bbc.co.uk/1/hi/magazine/4619063.stm

www.straightdope.com/columns/read/831/why-does-the-moon-appear-bigger-near-the-horizon

How icicles are formed: www.sciencedaily.com/videos/2007/0202-why_icicles_are_long_and_thin.htm

Perhaps the world's longest icicle: www.metro.co.uk/news/816123-at-27-foot-is-this-the-worlds-biggest-icicle

Russia's deadly icicles: http://news.bbc.co.uk/1/hi/world/europe/1219713.stm

The history of icicle-related deaths: http://gogreentravelgreen.com/green-travel-stories/10-chilling-tales-of-people-killed-by-icicles/

All things Easy Rider: http://easyridermovie.blogspot.com/ and http://tazrider.tripod.com/easyrider.html

The runaway tube train: www.bbc.co.uk/news/uk-england-10964766

The runaway train in Olympia:

www.historylink.org/index.cfm?DisplayPage=output.cfm&file_id=7929

The incident behind the film: www.toledoblade.com/

Movies/2010/11/12/Hollywood-widens-truth-gauge-in-runaway-train-flick.html

Genevieve tribute site: www.donbrockway.com/genevieve.htm
Thanks to the London Transport Museum for information on trams www.ltmuseum.co.uk

Details of the film: www.imdb.com/title/tt0059800/trivia
Information on the Rocket Belt: www.rocketbelt.nl
The Martin Jetpack: www.martinjetpack.com

Information on the film: www.imdb.com/title/tt0017925
A detailed review of the film: www.dvdsavant.com/s3069gene.html
Expert opinion on wheel slip: http://answers.yahoo.com/question/index?qid=20090728183017AAKJye5

Articles on the history of the Hejaz Railway: www.arabnews.com/?page=21&section=0&article=76563&d=23&m=1&y=200
www.saudiaramcoworld.com/issue/196505/pilgrim.s.road.htm
The geology of deserts: www.nps.gov/whsa/naturescience/upload/Geology%20of%20Sand%20Dunes.pdf

Details on Duel: http://duelmovie.webatu.com/
The surviving Duel truck: www.stlouisdumptrucks.com/Duel/index.html
Truck racing: www.britishtruckracing.co.uk/
The world's fastest truck: www.techeblog.com/index.php/tech-gadget/feature-world-s-fastest-truck-reaches-376mph-with-video-

The filming of the subway grate scene: www.cinemaretro.com/index.php?/archives/2484-photographing-marilyn-monroe-

in-the-seven-year-itch.html

Video of Joshua Allen Harris' inflatable art: www.youtube.com/
watch?v=PH6xCT2aTSo

New York's new subway grates: http://secondavenuesagas.
com/2010/04/16/new-raised-storm-grates-earn-architectural-
praise/

Information on and video of the world's longest train: www.
paklinks.com/gs/video-gallery/379066-worlds-longest-
freight-train-from-the-guinnes-book-of-world-records.html

The invention of the autopilot: www.century-of-flight.freeola.
com/Aviation history/evolution of technology/autopilot.htm

How autopilots work: http://science.howstuffworks.com/
transport/flight/modern/autopilot.htm

The history of Dogtown and the Z-Boys: www.angelfire.com/ca/
alva3/spin.html

http://skateboard.about.com/od/boardscience/a/
DogtownHistory.htm

Interview with Sara Gruen: www.sandiegoreader.com/
news/2006/nov/16/water-elephants-novel/

Etymology of redlighting: http://wordcraft.infopop.cc/eve/
forums/a/tpc/f/932607094/m/4051061414

Real-life redlighting: www.circushistory.org/Bandwagon/
bw-1963Sep.htm

How to jump from a train: The Worst-case Scenario Travel
Handbook by David Borgenicht and Joshua Piven (Chronicle
Books, 2001)Skateboarding tricks: www.board-crazy.co.uk/
tricktionary.php

Everything you want to know about falling out of the sky: www.
greenharbor.com/fffolder/ffresearch.html

The history of sniping: www.armchairgeneral.com/forums/
showthread.php?t=16961&page=2

Report on Corporal Harrison's record-breaking shot: www.
dailymail.co.uk/news/article-1270414/British-sniper-sets-
new-sharpshooting-record-1-54-mile-double-Taliban-kill.
html#ixzz0p3KRAR31

Sonic weapons: www.guardian.co.uk/science/2005/nov/08/
g2.weaponstechnology

http://news.scotsman.com/scotland/Rights-row-over-sonic-
deterrent.6413547.jp

http://science.howstuffworks.com/lrad.htm/printable

Death by sound: www.straightdope.com/columns/read/2298/
can-a-noise-be-loud-enough-to-kill-you

Pistol shrimps: www.dailymail.co.uk/sciencetech/
article-1085398/Deadly-pistol-shrimp-stuns-prey-sound-
loud-Concorde-UK-waters.html

Making of the film: www.imdb.com/title/tt0073341/
The Sporting Arms and Ammunition Manufacturers'
Institute: www.saami.org

Info on the cooking off of cartridges: www.cartridgecollectors.
org/faq.htm and www.thehighroad.org/archive/index.php/t-
278523.html

Discussion of flintlocks in colonial America: www.
armchairgeneral.com/forums/showthread.
php?t=16961&page=2

How flintlocks work: http://science.howstuffworks.com/
flintlock.htm

How flamethrowers work: http://science.howstuffworks.com/
flamethrower.htm/printable

Everything to do with knife-throwing and home of the UK's
only Knife Club: www.knifethrowing.co.uk
Note: Before even thinking about throwing a knife, please visit
this website for guidance on knife safety and the law.

Everything about Nelson: www.aboutnelson.co.uk
The Royal Naval Museum in Portsmouth has an interactive
Trafalgar! exhibition, putting you on the gundeck of HMS
Victory: www.royalnavalmuseum.org

Report on Marquel's death: http://news.sky.com/skynews/Home/
World-News/Marquel-Peters-Stray-Bullet-Kills-Boy-Three-
Miles-Away-In-Decatur-Church-Near-Atlanta-Georgia/
Article/201001115513798
Description of the US Army tests: www.loadammo.com/Topics/
March01.htm

Various articles and information on guns, bullets and hunting:
www.sixguns.com/crew/sskbullets.htm
www.gunsandammo.com

http://findarticles.com/p/articles/mi_m0BTT/is_177_29/ai_
n14816284/pg_2/?tag=content;col1
www. www.bigfivehq.com

The Newton's laws and the conservation of momentum: www.
brianmac.co.uk/biomechanics.htm
Discussion on shotgun power: www.shotgunworld.com/bbs/
viewtopic.php?f=2&t=30167
All about ninjas: http://asianhistory.about.com/od/warsinasia/p/
NinjaProfile.htm
http://www.h2g2.com/approved_entry/A575642

Information on the film: www.imdb.com/title/tt0087507/

The history of the Stuka: www.vectorsite.net/avstuka.html

Discussions about whistling bombs: www.answerbag.co.uk/q_
view/41209#ixzz0suUPyy8g

www.ww2talk.com/forum/

http://tvtropes.org/pmwiki/pmwiki.php/Main/BombWhistle

Doppler's discovery: http://www.h2g2.com/approved_entry/
A827372

The Chase Distillery in Hereford produces the UK's only potato
vodka: www.chasedistillery.co.uk

Information on poitín: http://en.wikipedia.org/wiki/
Poit%C3%ADn

The dangers of drinking lighter fluid: www.thesite.org/
drinkanddrugs/askthesiteqandas/drinkanddrugsqandas/
lethallighterfluid

www.wrongdiagnosis.com/c/chemical_poisoning_lighter_fluid/
intro.htm

www.drugs.com/enc/lighter-fluid.html

Information about the film: www.imdb.com/title/tt0094336/

The story of Vivian MacKerrell: www.richard-e-grant.com/
archives/the-real-withnail

Caviar and how to serve it:

www.jamesbondlifestyle.com/product/beluga-caviar

www.tjbd.co.uk/james-bond-food.htm

www.barkeeper.co.uk/3page.asp?menu=117&page=311&Subp
age=38

The history and manufacture of golf balls:

www.golfball-guide.de/knowledge.htm

How to cook meat: http://missvickie.com/howto/meat/tough.
html

Oscar's story: www.guardian.co.uk/uk/2008/sep/06/
animalwelfare

Everything about chillis: http://ushotstuff.com/

The world's hottest chillis: www.msnbc.msn.com/id/20058096/

How chilli sauce can kill: www.newscientist.com/blogs/
shortsharpscience/2008/09/how-chilis-can-kill.html

History of wine: www.arenaflowers.com/wine_club_online/
history_of_wine

A chronology of chronology: www.historyworld.net/wrldhis/
PlainTextHistories.asp?historyid=ac33

How to make a Red Eye: www.drinkstreet.com/searchresults.cgi
?drinkid=1126&drinkname=category:20

Hangover cures: http://www.h2g2.com/approved_entry/
A103140

How bacon sandwiches work: www.telegraph.co.uk/science/
science-news/5118283/Bacon-sandwich-really-does-cure-a-
hangover.html

Banana skins in all different media: www.tvtropes.org/pmwiki/
pmwiki.php/Main/BananaPeel

Testing slipperiness in Sheffield: http://kn.theiet.org/
communities/tribology/blog/banana.cfm

Details of the film: www.imdb.com/title/tt0069847/

Different aphrodisiacs examined: www.dailymail.co.uk/femail/
article-158927/The-secret-aphrodisiacs-food.html

http://news.nationalgeographic.com/
news/2006/02/0214_060214_valentines.html

www.forbes.com/2003/09/10/cx_ns_0910healthintro.html

The history of absinthe: www.straightdope.com/columns/
read/2322/was-the-legendary-liqueur-absinthe-
hallucinogenic

The history of the martini: http://ezinearticles.com/?The-

History-of-the-Martini&id=336022

Martinis at the Dukes Hotel: http://laissezfare.wordpress.
com/2009/07/01/dukes-bar-the-martini-that-inspired-ian-
fleming/

The University of Western Ontario study: www.bmj.com/
content/319/7225/1600.full

Margarita history: www.imbibe.com/article/once-upon-time-in-
mexico

Brain freeze experiment: http://www.bmj.com/
content/314/7091/1364

Brain freeze causes: www.wisegeek.com/what-causes-brain-
freeze.htm

Mastodons and mammoths: http://dinosaurs.about.com/od/
mesozoicmammals/a/elephants.htm

Eating prehistoric animals: www.straightdope.com/columns/
read/2725/prehistoric-its-whats-for-dinner

Details on the film: www.imdb.com/title/tt0052618/

Why we burp: www.corecharity.org.uk/Windy-symptoms-
Flatulence-belching-bloating-and-breaking-wind.html

The world's loudest burper: www.myspace.com/burperking

Dining etiquette: http://www.h2g2.com/approved_entry/
A354782

A swallow's carrying ability in depth: www.style.org/
unladenswallow/

How to tickle trout: www.woodlands.co.uk/blog/wild-food/
trout-tickling/

Fishing advice and regulations: www.environment-agency.gov.
uk/homeandleisure/recreation/fishing/default.aspx

Why we have wisdom teeth: www.popsci.com/scitech/
   article/2009-08/do-animals-have-wisdom-teeth
Horses and wolf teeth: www.horseandhound.co.uk/horse-care-
   index/1370/99729.html
The Vatican's favourite films: http://old.usccb.org/movies/
   vaticanfilms.shtml
All things pigeon: www.nationalpigeonassociation.co.uk
More pigeon facts: www.bbc.co.uk/nature/life/Rock_Pigeon
Cheating birds: www.guardian.co.uk/books/2001/may/19/
   scienceandnature.books
Swan divorce reported: www.metro.co.uk/news/810215-swan-
   divorce-surprises-bird-experts

Crystal the "smoking" monkey: http://www.webcitation.
   org/5z7ybYavz
www.usatoday.com/life/movies/news/2011-05-31-crystal-
   monkey-hangover_n.htm
Charlie the chimp: www.bbc.co.uk/news/11484057
Po the snake: www.metro.co.uk/weird/811367-the-snake-whos-
   hooked-on-cigarettes#ixzz1ODrxmoIw
The beagle experiment: www.sourcewatch.org/index.
   php?title=Smoking_beagles
Animal addictions: http://news.softpedia.com/news/Animals-
   on-Drugs-41500.shtml
Drunken monkeys: www.telegraph.co.uk/science/
   science-news/3291518/Quest-for-alcohol-gene-sets-monkeys-
   on-binge.html

Leeches and how to remove them: www.wildmadagascar.org/
   overview/leeches.html
Pufferfish facts:
www.nytimes.com/2009/12/22/science/22creature.html and
   www.fugufish.info/
Tetrodotoxin facts: http://en.wikipedia.org/wiki/Tetrodotoxin

How we see: http://askabiologist.asu.edu/content/seeing-color

How bulls see: www.thenakedscientists.com/HTML/content/questions/question/1336/

How mantis shrimps see: www.wired.com/wiredscience/2009/10/mantis-shrimp-eyes/#ixzz0uz5VY1mA

How to care for an iguana that's lost its tail: www.greenigsociety.org/tailloss.htm

Details of the film: www.imdb.com/title/tt0478304

Dinosaur misconceptions: http://paleobiology.si.edu/dinosaurs/info/misconceptions/mis_4.html

What dinosaurs might have looked like: http://discovermagazine.com/2000/sep/featdino

Dinosaur colour revealed: www.nhm.ac.uk/about-us/news/2010/january/dinosaur-colour-revealed-for-first-time54856.html

Maggot Therapy: A Handbook of Maggot-Assisted Wound Healing by Wim Fleischmann, M.D., Martin Grassberger, M.D., Ph.D. and Ronald Sherman, M.D., M.Sc. (Thieme, 2004)

John Carradine's career: www.imdb.com/name/nm0001017/

Information on elephants and their graveyards: www.sheldrickwildlifetrust.org/html/debate.html

www.animalinfo.org/species/loxoafri.htm

www.upali.ch/teeth_en

www.guardian.co.uk/education/2006/jan/10/workinprogress.highereducation

The megladon discussed: www.livescience.com/animals/050426_great_white.html

Shark stuff: http://animals.nationalgeographic.com/animals/
   fish/great-white-shark.html
www.jawshark.com

FBI fingerprints manual: www.fbi.gov/hq/cjisd/takingfps.html
Report on migrants who burn off their prints: www.dailymail.
   co.uk/news/article-1202009/Bloody-siege-Calais-The-
   violent-new-breed-migrants-let-stop-coming-Britain.
   html#ixzz0Um7BOWRi
Report on Mexican surgeon: www.smh.com.au/
   news/world/surgeon-jailed-for-removing-fingerpri
   nts/2008/02/14/1202760429686.html

Observations on the Toxic Effects of Cordite by J. S. Weiner and
   M. L. Thomson (BMJ Publishing Group Ltd) sourced at www.
   oem.bmj.com/cgi/reprint/4/4/205
Symptoms of nitroglycerin overdose reported: www.drugs.com/
   enc/nitroglycerin-overdose.html
Report of Viktor Yushchenko's poisoning: http://news.bbc.
   co.uk/1/hi/health/4041321.stm

Teleportation explored: www.physics.org/explorelink.asp?id=95
   9&q=ifs&currentpage=1&age=0&knowledge=0&item=6

Wormholes explored: www.livescience.com/technology/080214-
   jumper-movie.html

Information on the film: www.imdb.com/title/tt0032155/
The history of gold: www.goldipedia.gold.org/history_and_
   culture
How to detect real gold: www.gerrardsonline.co.uk/history_of_
   gold.htm

The truth about Charlestown: www.boston.com/news/local/

massachusetts/articles/2010/09/18/afflecks_new_film_is_the_ talk_of_the_townies/

The world's most dangerous cities: http://urbantitan.com/10-most-dangerous-cities-in-the-world-in-2011/

The world's leading card-cheating website: http://cardshark.us

Takuo Toda's record: www.guardian.co.uk/world/2009/dec/27/ paper-plane-flight-record-japan

Paper plane resources: www.paperplane.org/education.html

Paper plane in space: www.telegraph.co.uk/science/ space/8124611/Paper-aeroplane-launched-into-space-captures-breathtaking-images.html

Information on napalm: www.chm.bris.ac.uk/webprojects2001/ wright/napalm.htm

Interview with the author of the novel Fight Club: www.dvdtalk. com/interviews/chuck_palahniuk.html

Evidence of and theories on crucifixion: www.ncbi.nlm.nih.gov/ pmc/articles/PMC1420788/

www.museumstuff.com/learn/topics/crucifixion::sub::Details

Information on face transplants: http://health.howstuffworks. com/wellness/cosmetic-treatments/human-face-transplant. htm

www.bbc.co.uk/news/health-10765005

Sir Michael reveals his idea: http://news.bbc.co.uk/1/hi/ entertainment/7756288.stm

The Royal Society of Chemistry: www.rsc.org

The results of its competition: http://news.bbc.co.uk/1/hi/sci/ tech/7845533.stm

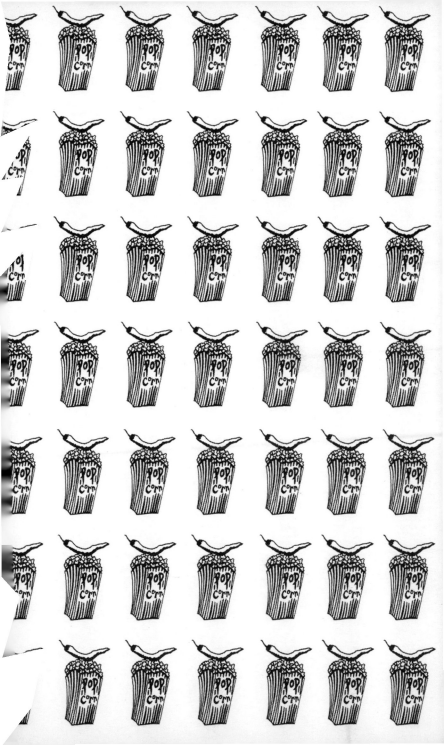